INTRODUCTION

In the beginning...before things like matter and trees, before cats and dogs or you and me, there was the **ENERGY**.

This Energy stretched from one end of the Universe to the other. It formed the very canvas of reality as we know it.

One day, the Energy decided to sing a song. The vibrations of this song created beautiful patterns. As they travelled throughout the Universe, these strings of energy would later condense into 3rd dimensional matter. Everything we see, taste, touch and feel is a child of that very special sound.

The following Mandalas are a tribute to that song. Known by Tibetan monks, shamans, mystics and artists throughout time, these patterns honor the fingerprint of the Universe. You may experience peace, tranquility and joy while coloring these images. Relax, these are normal side-effects. Consider this your moment of Zen.

I hope you have as much fun exploring these pages as my wife Karen has had creating them for you. **Enjoy**!

-Alex Karasz
2016

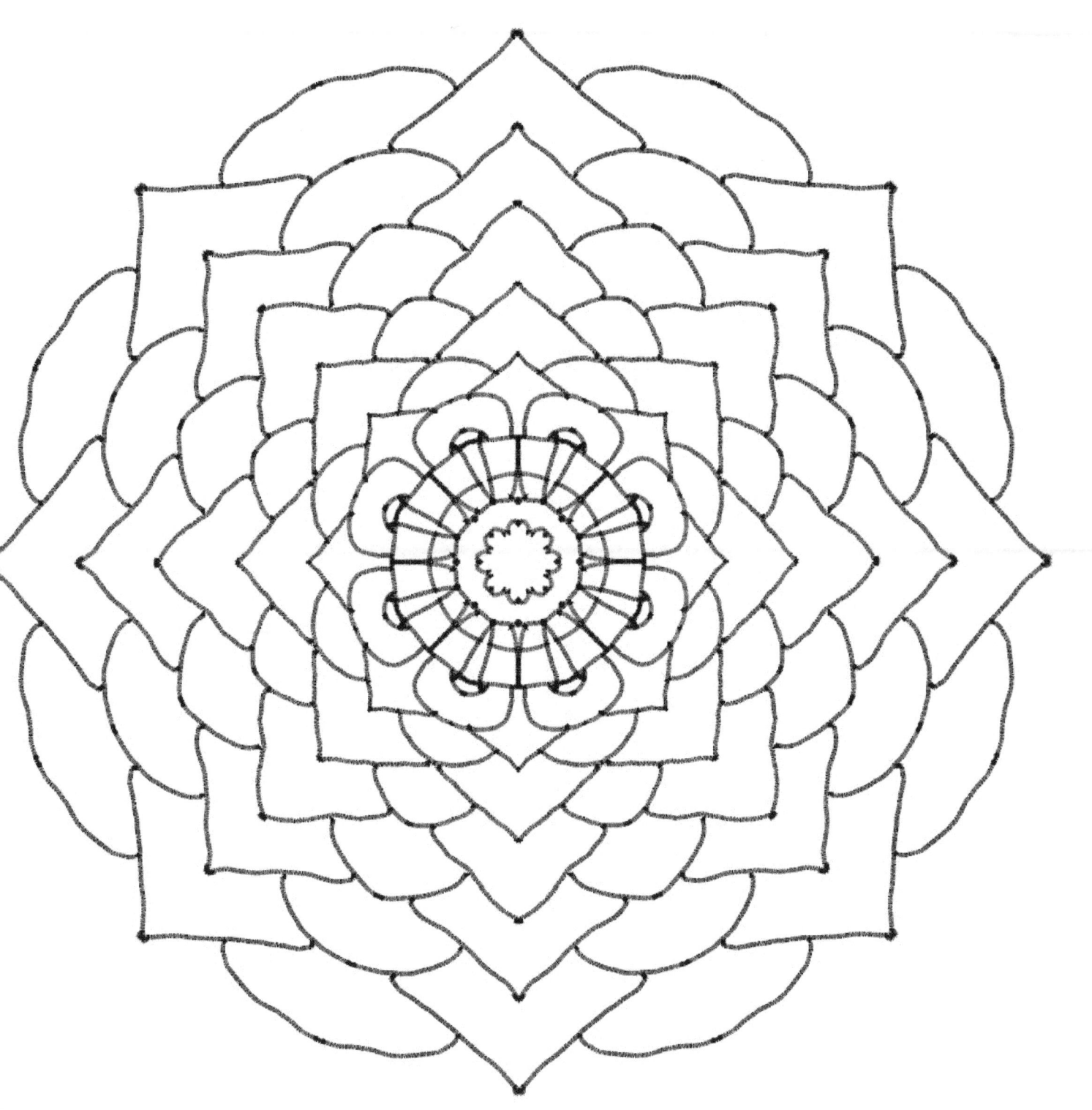

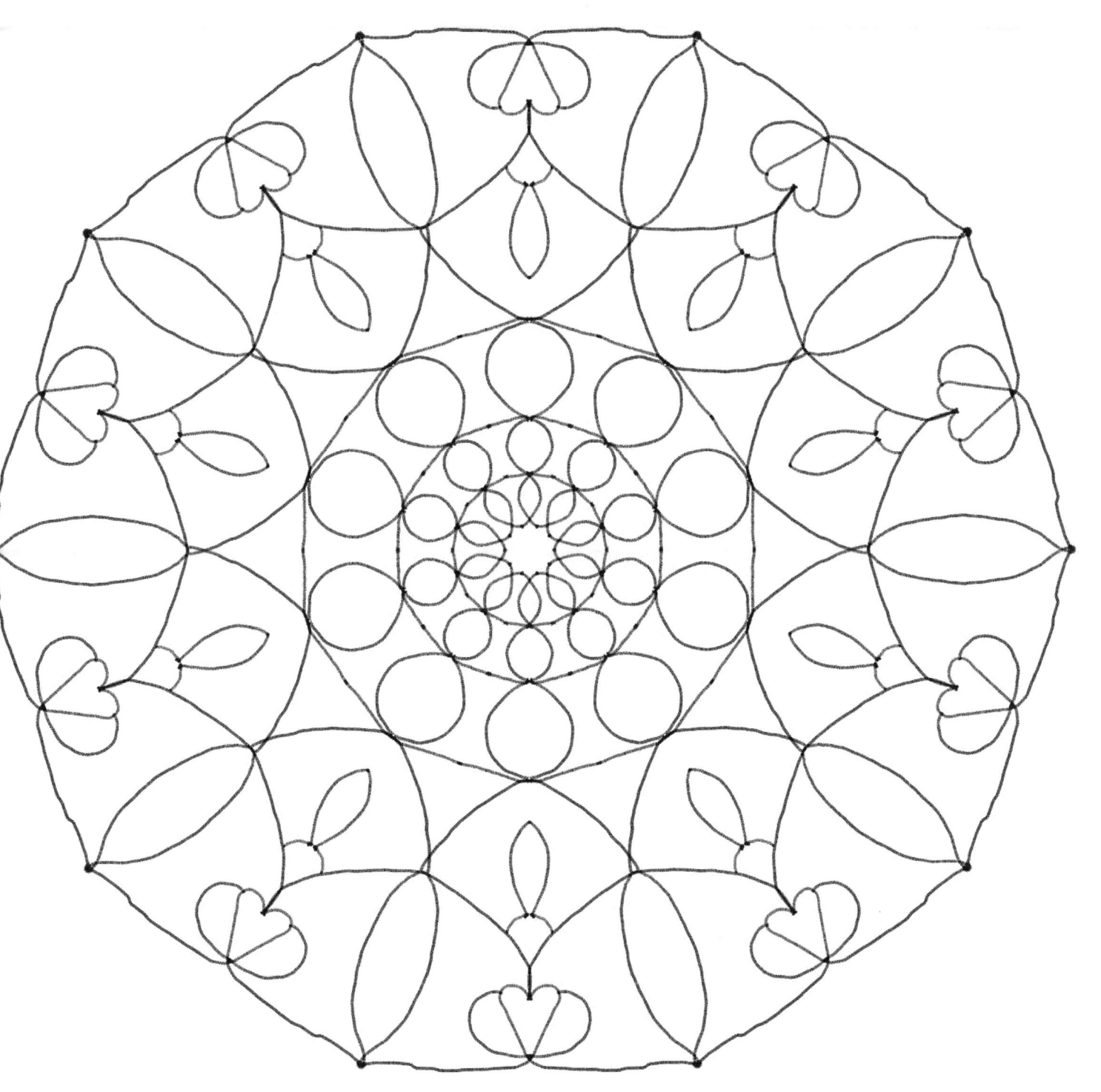

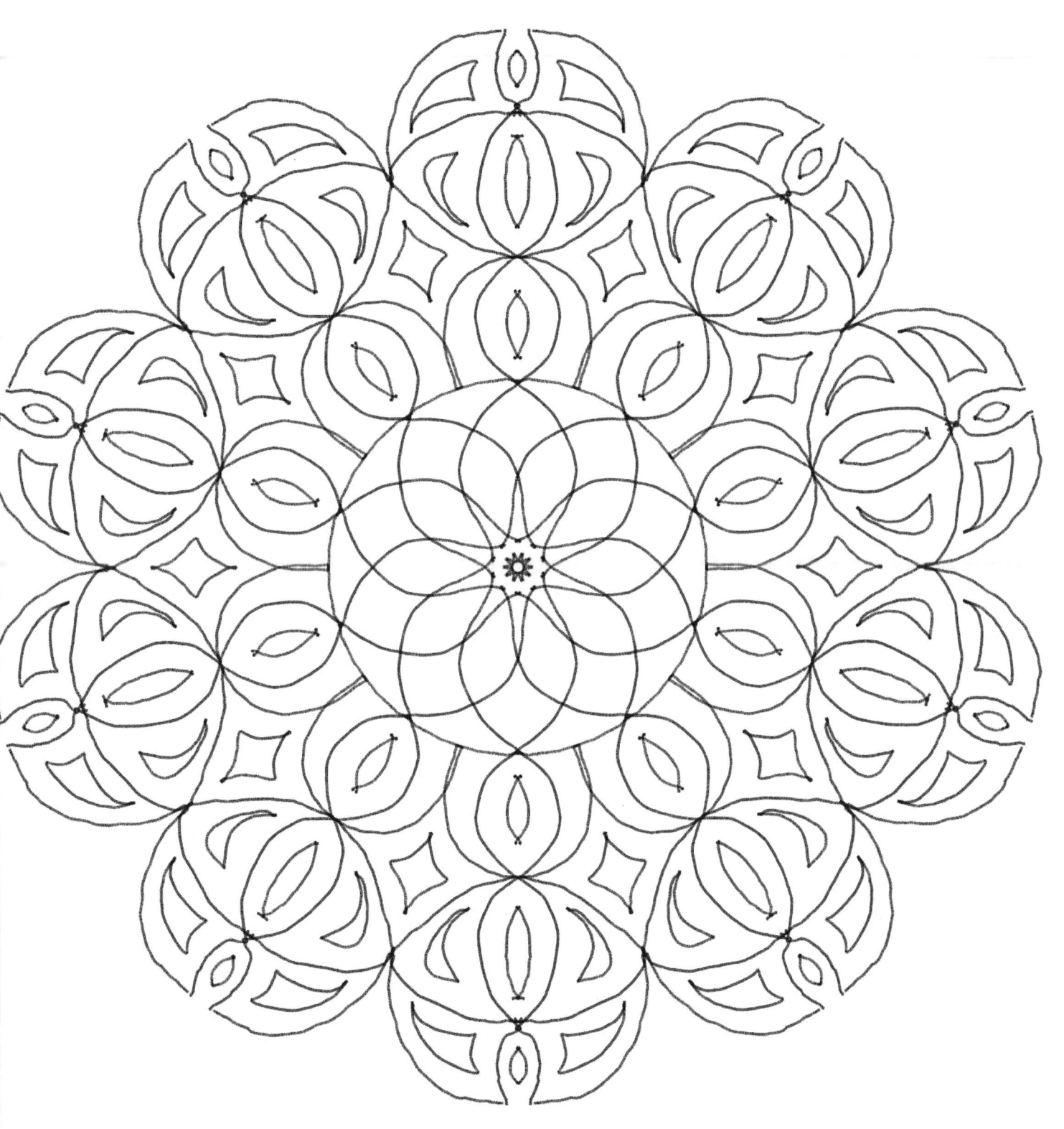

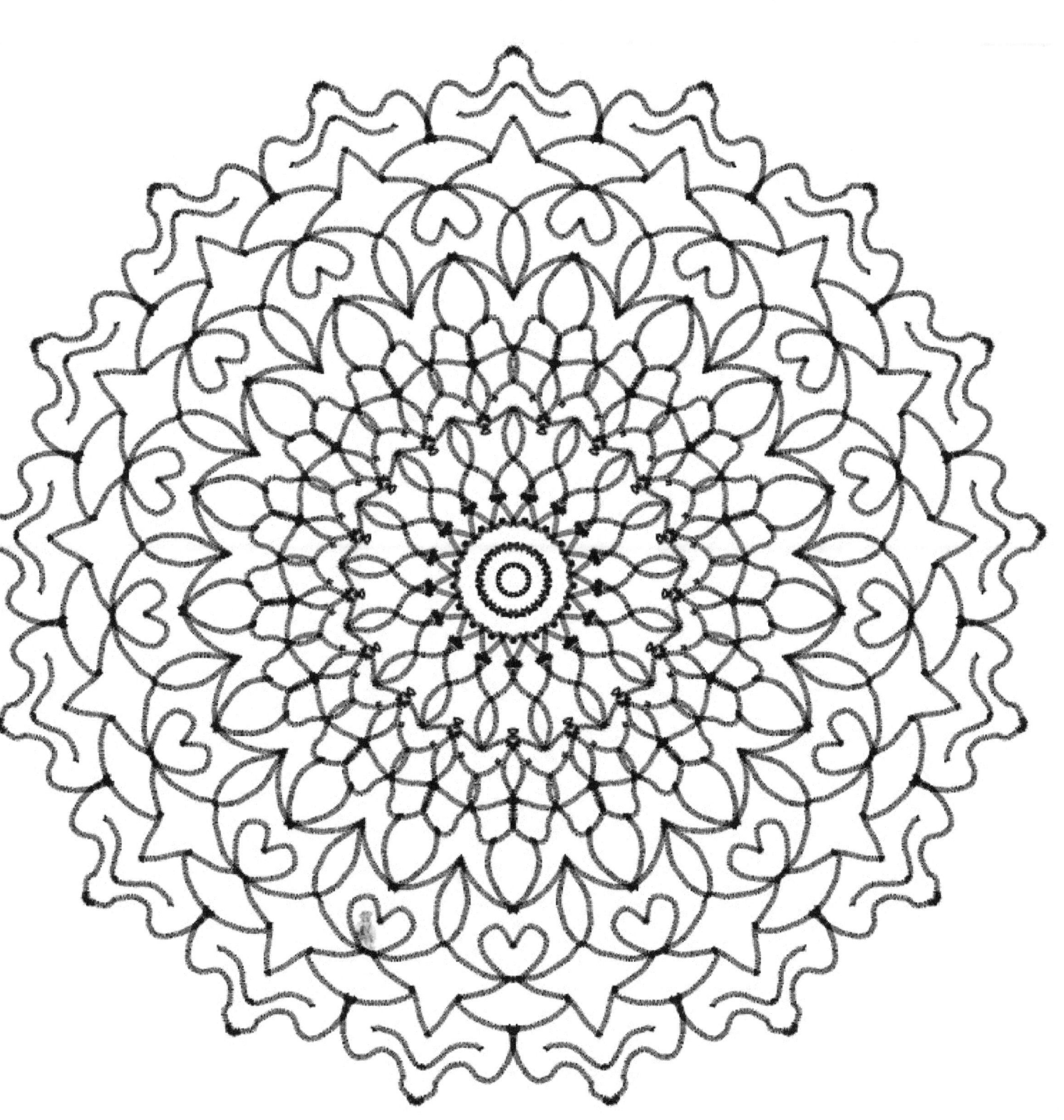

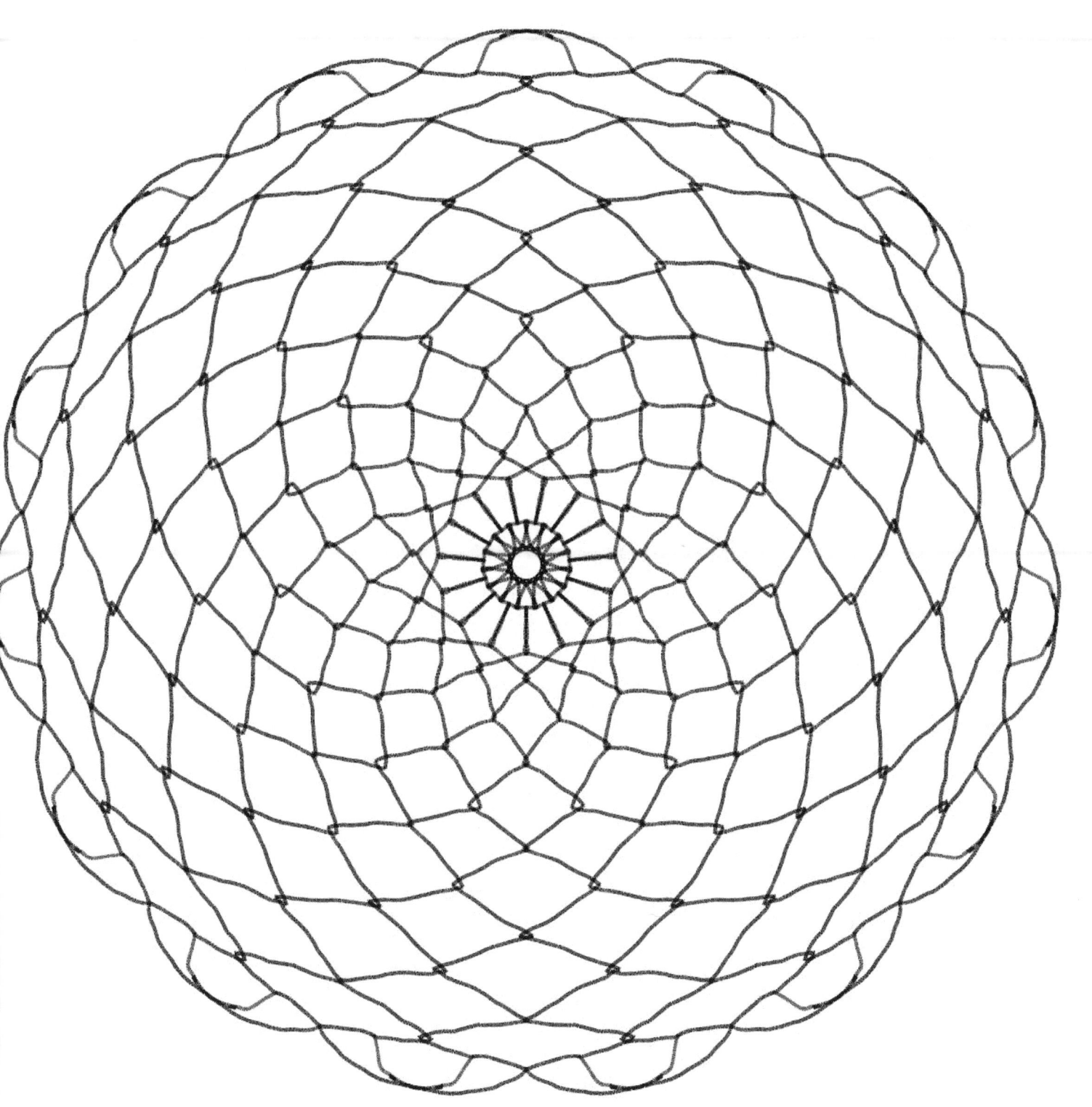

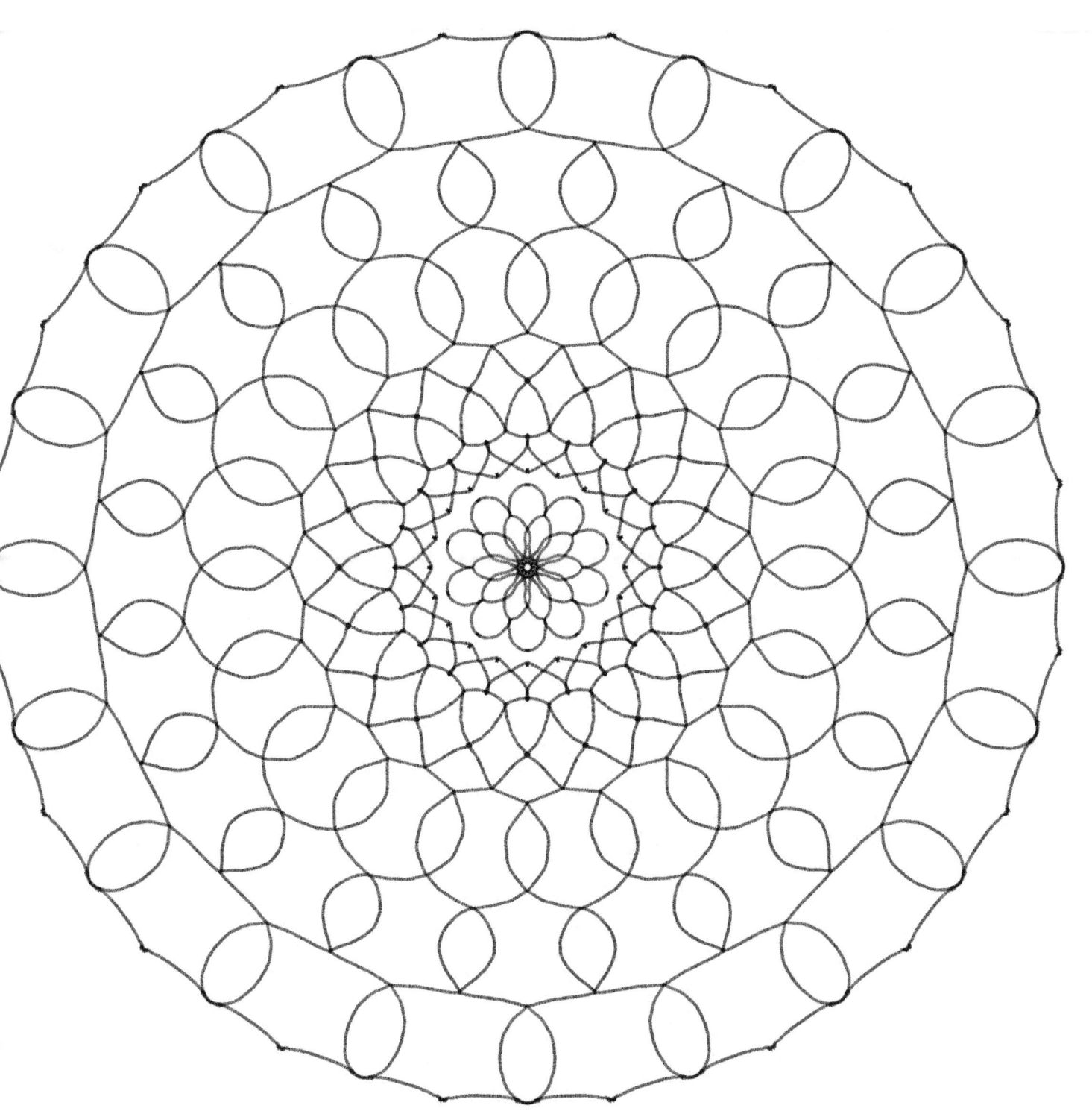

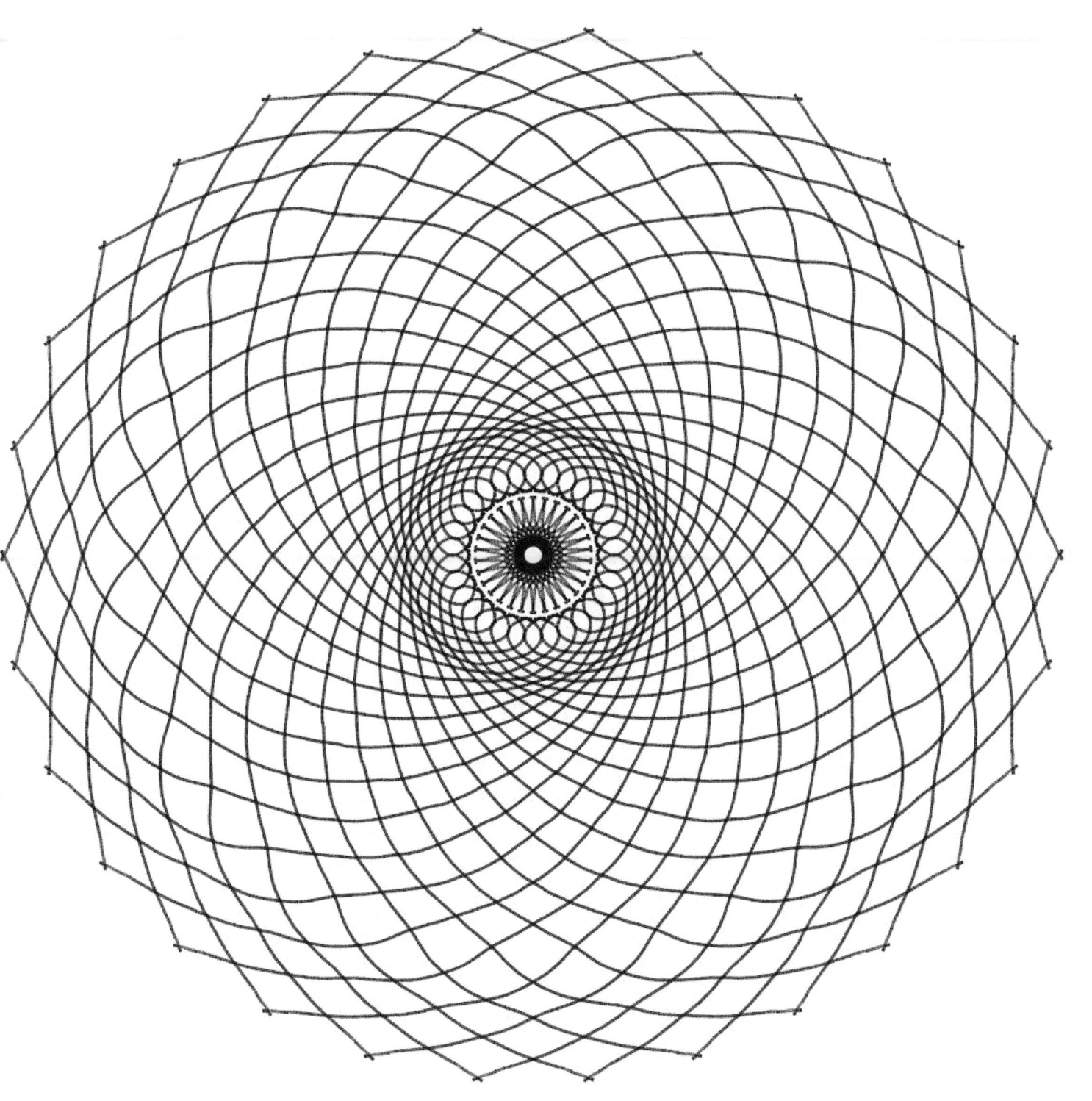

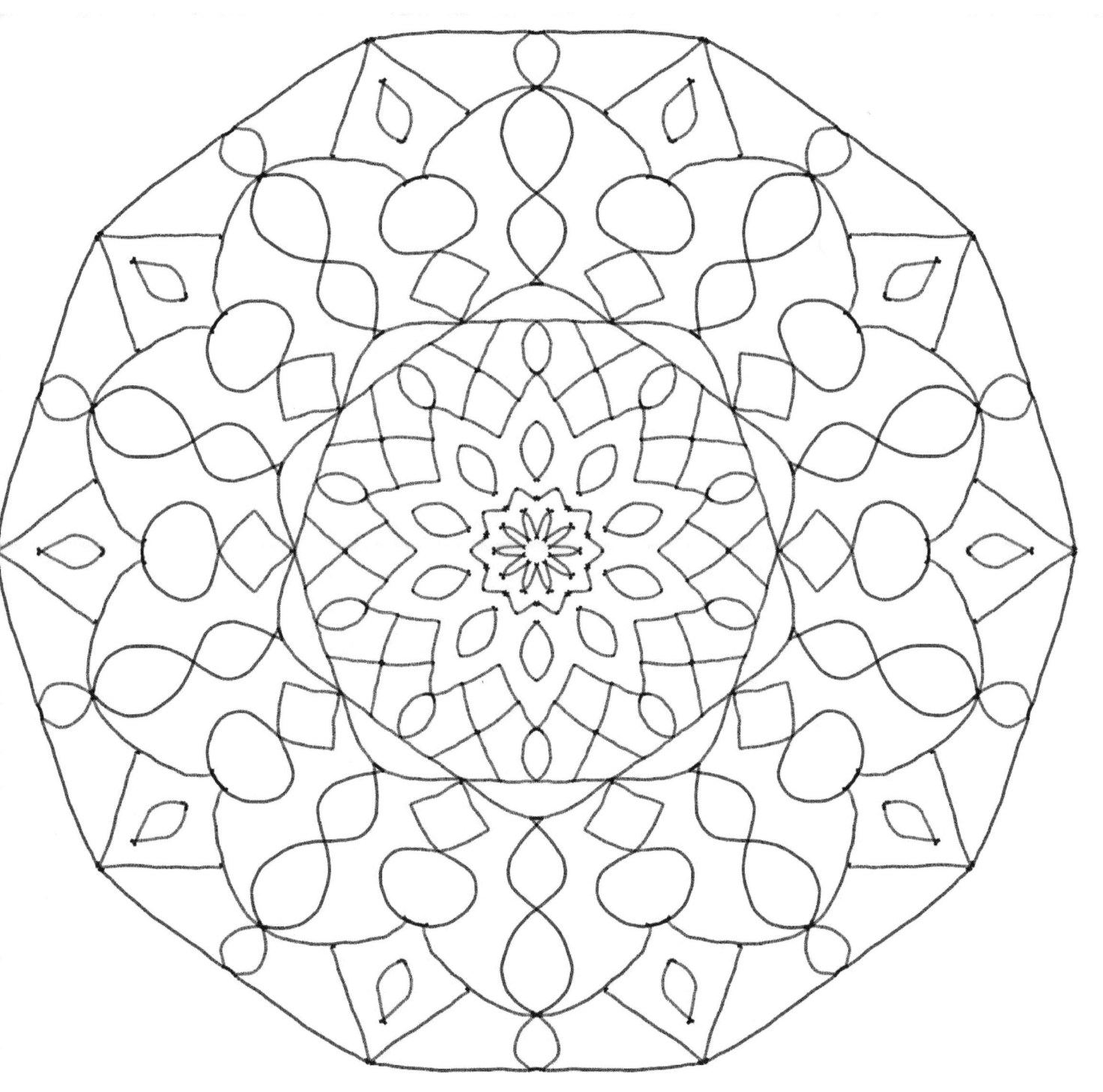

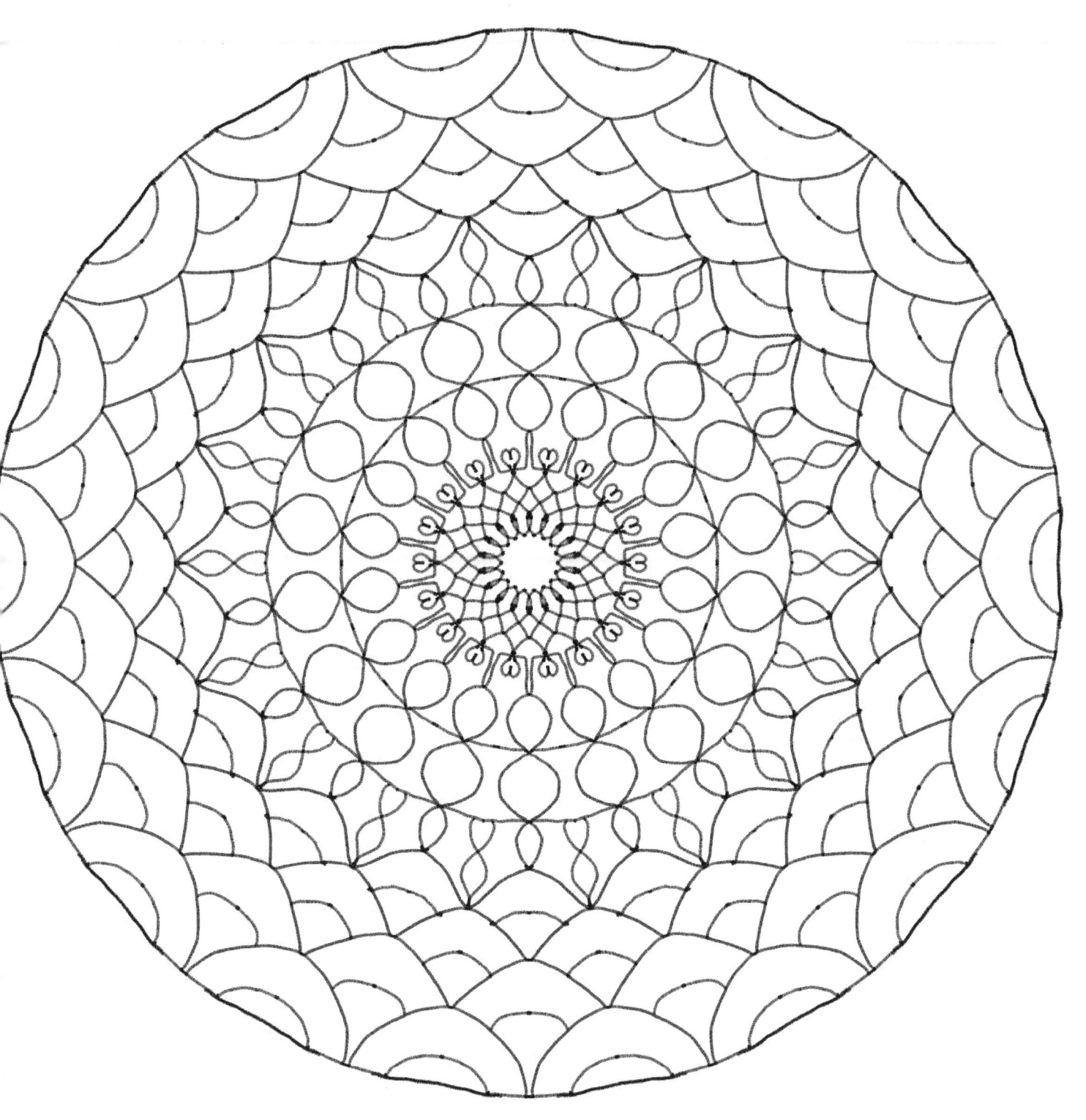

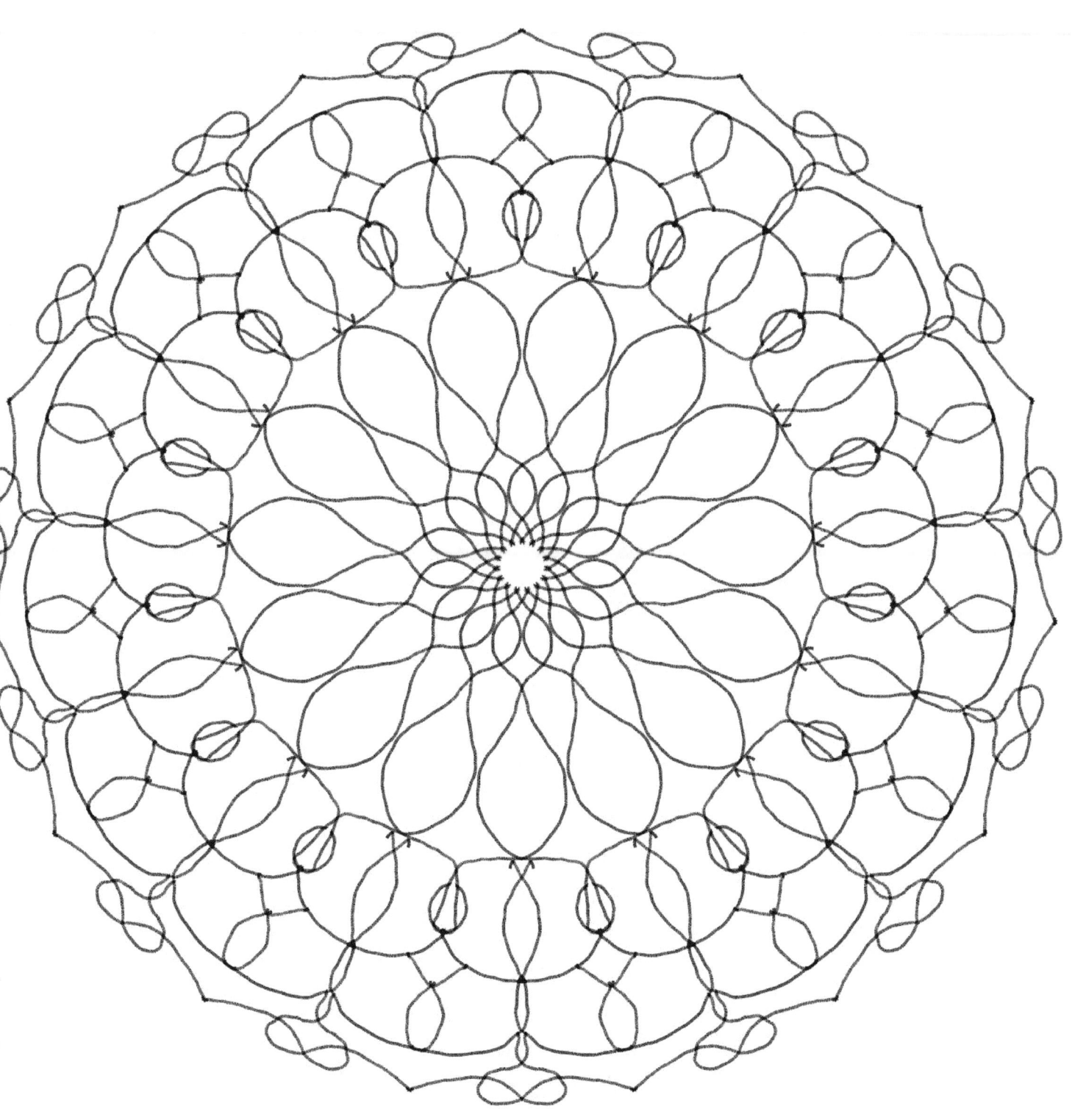

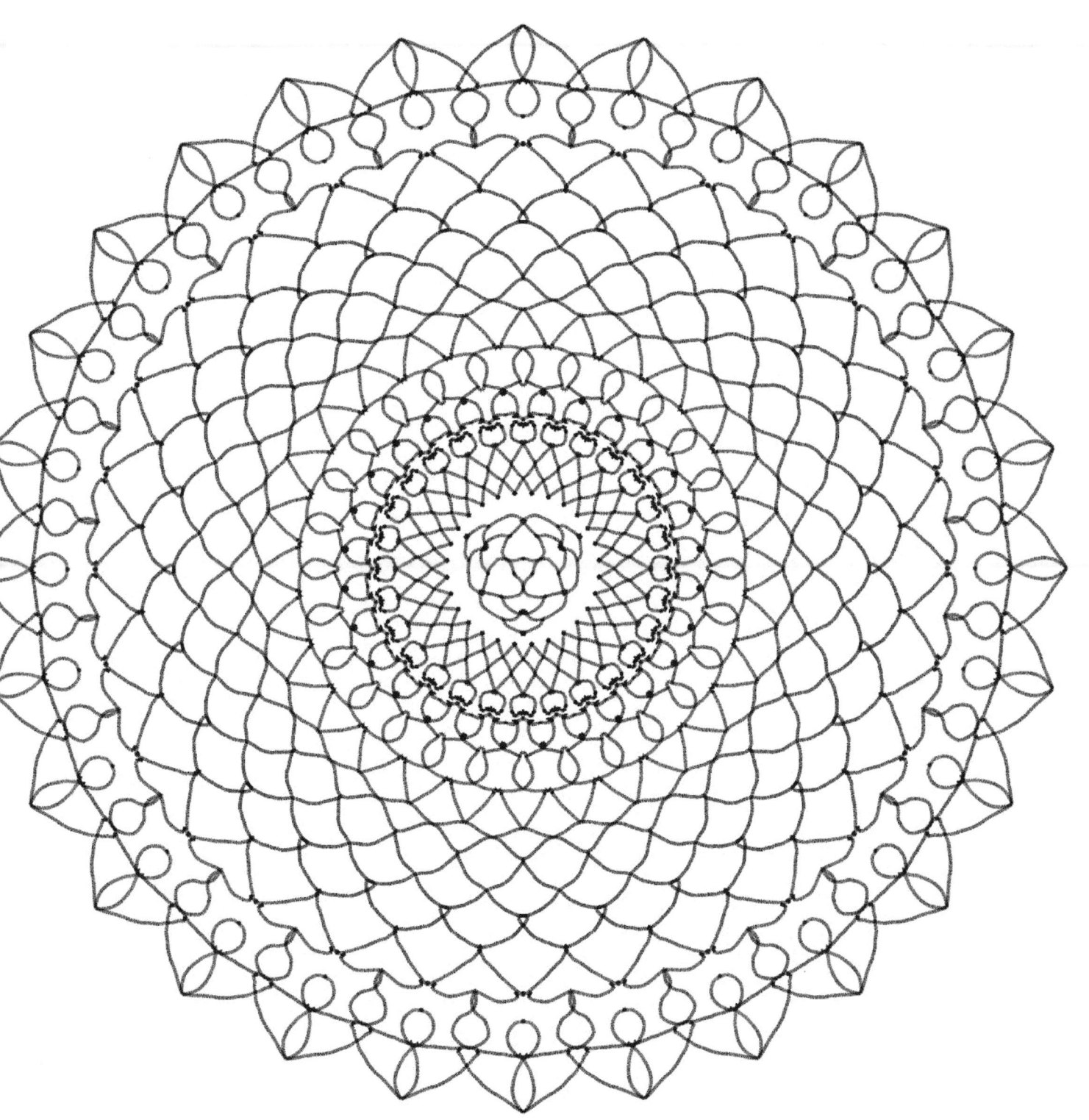

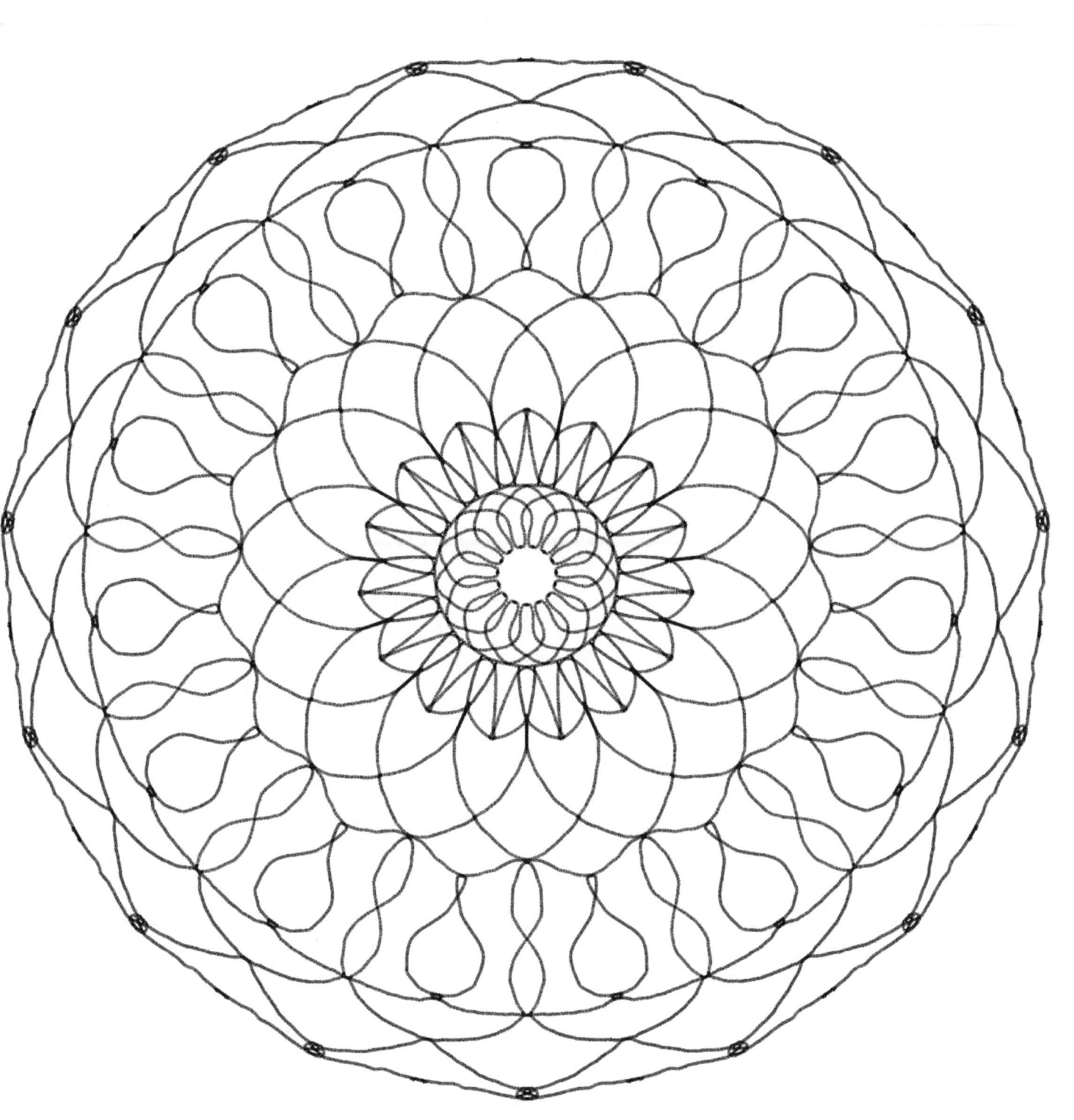

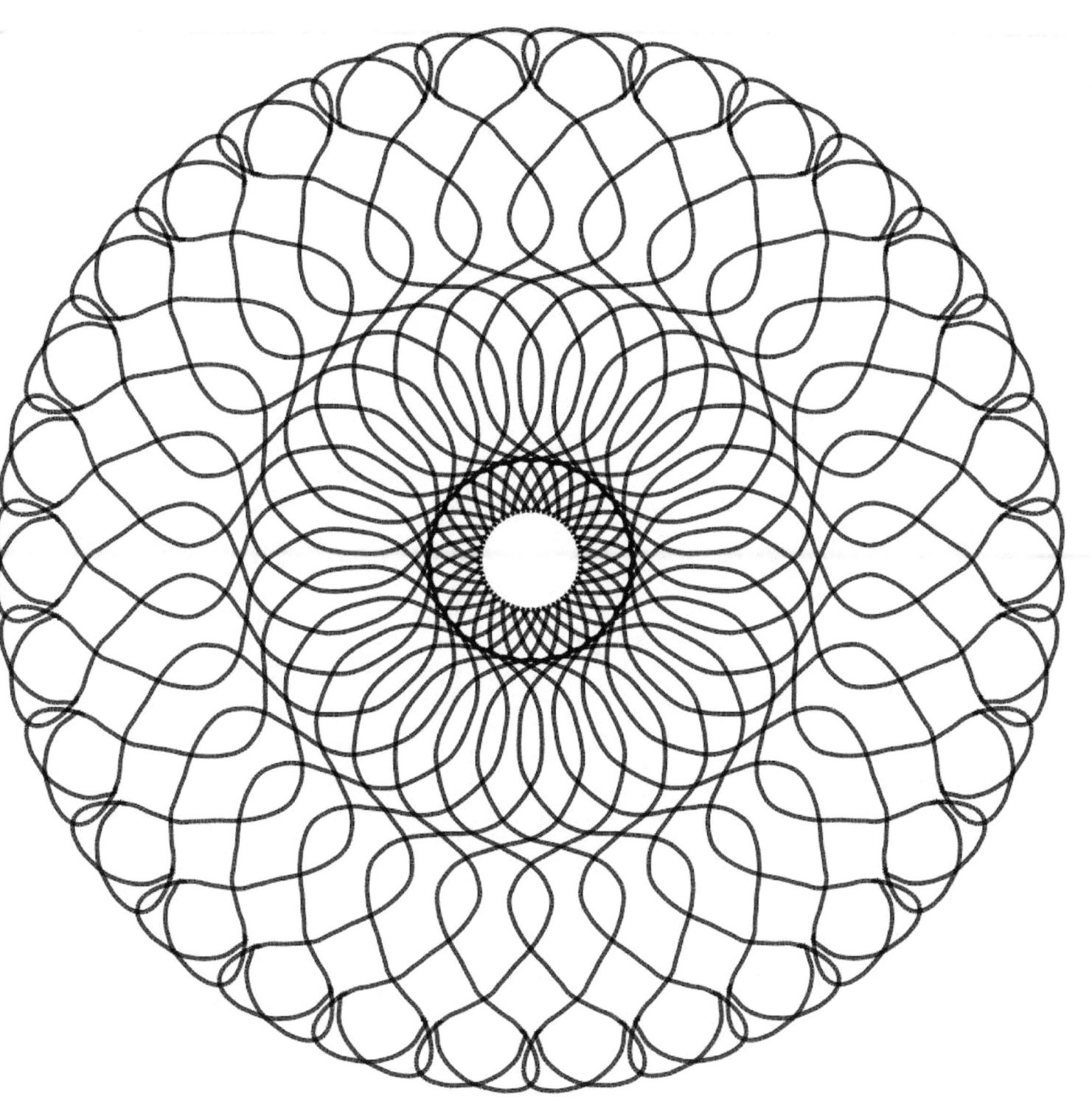

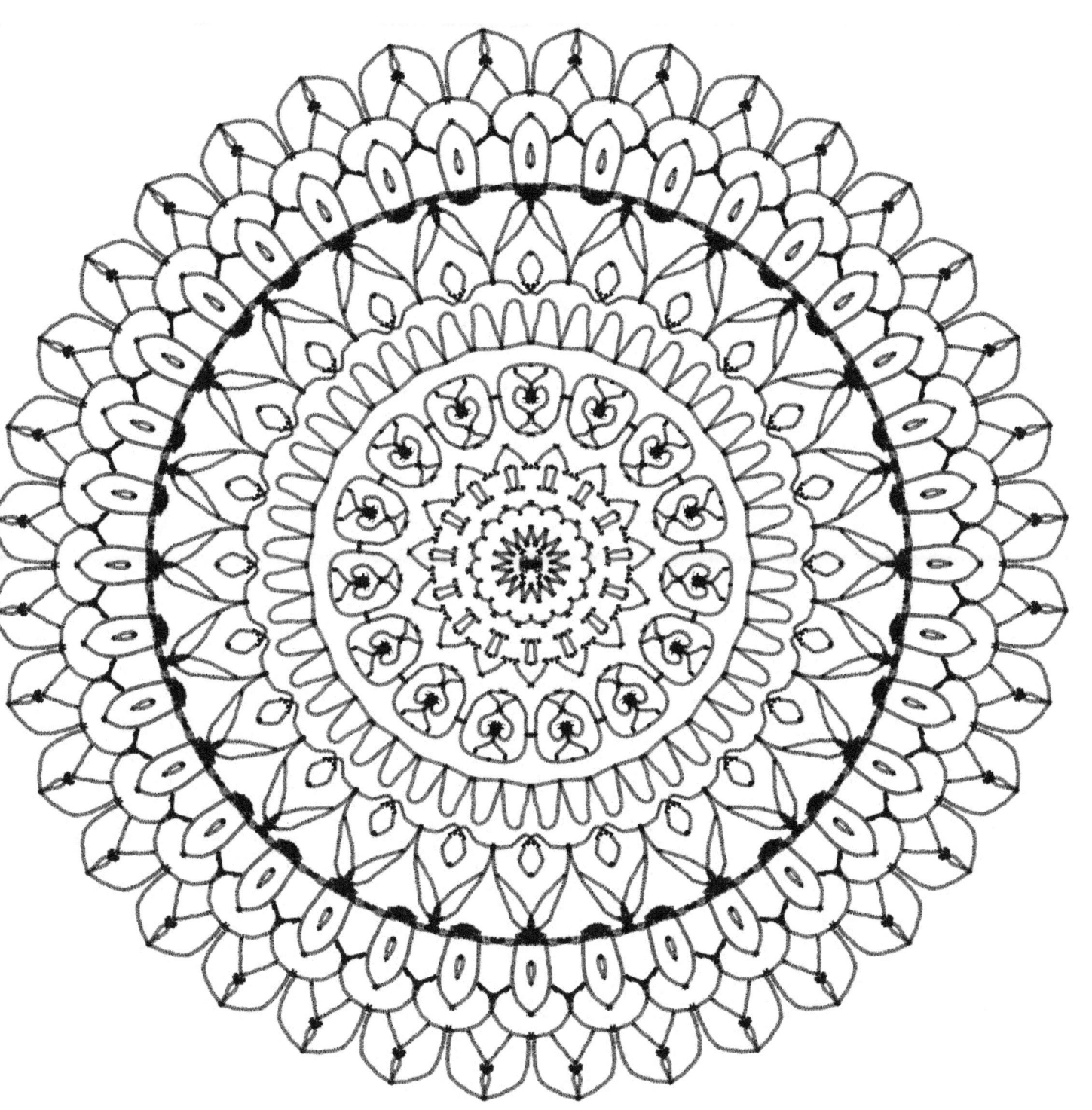

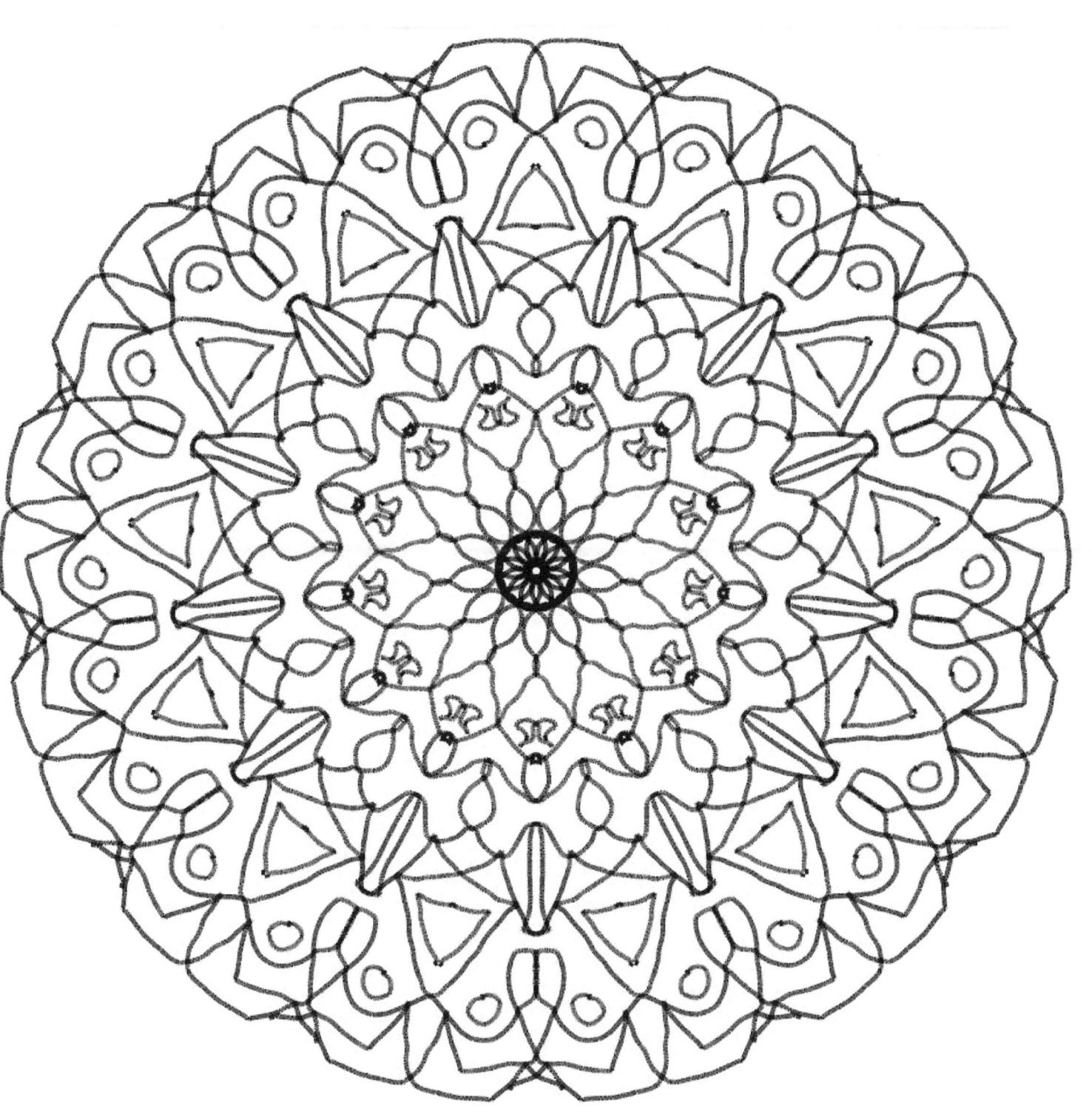

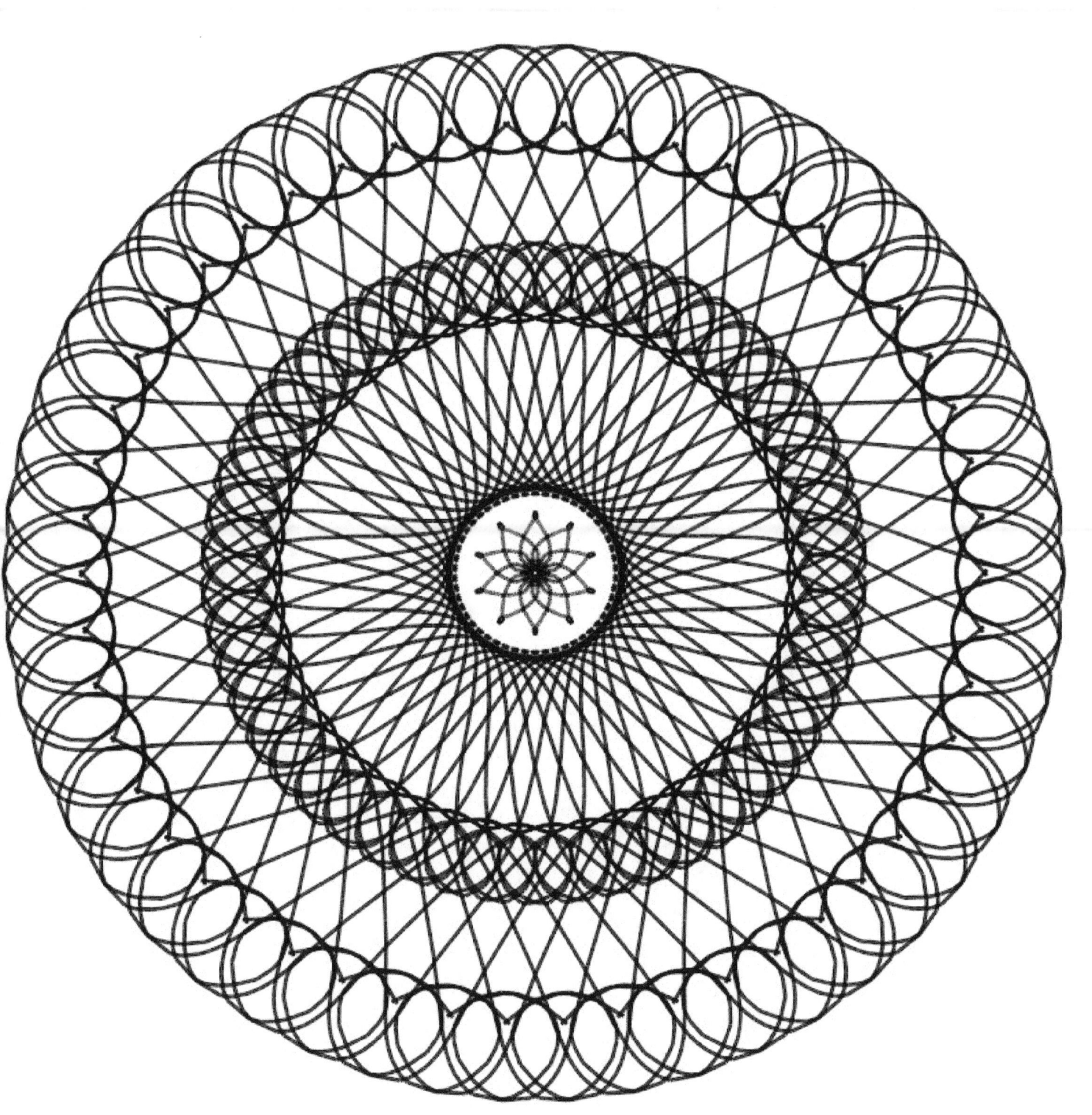

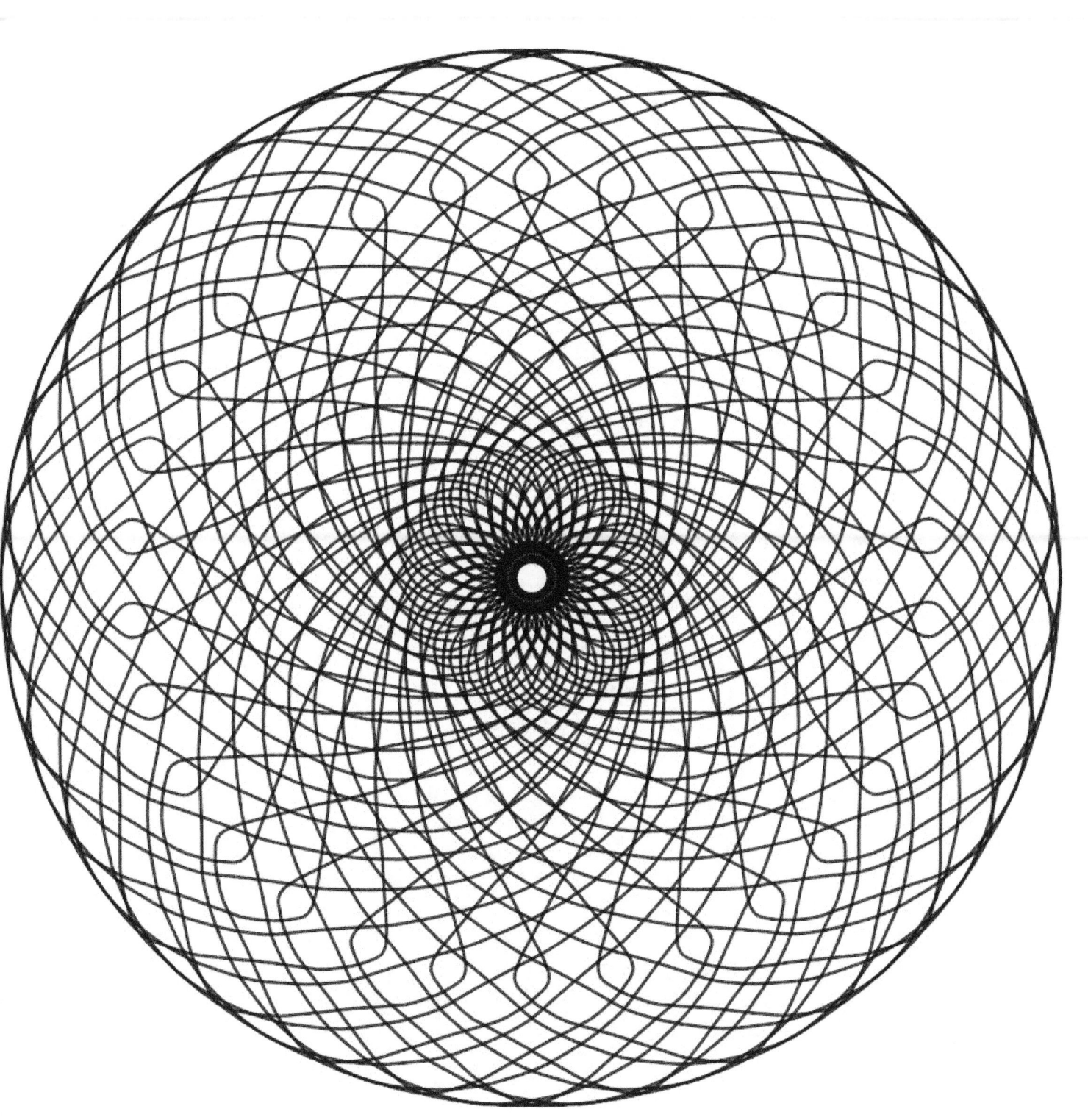

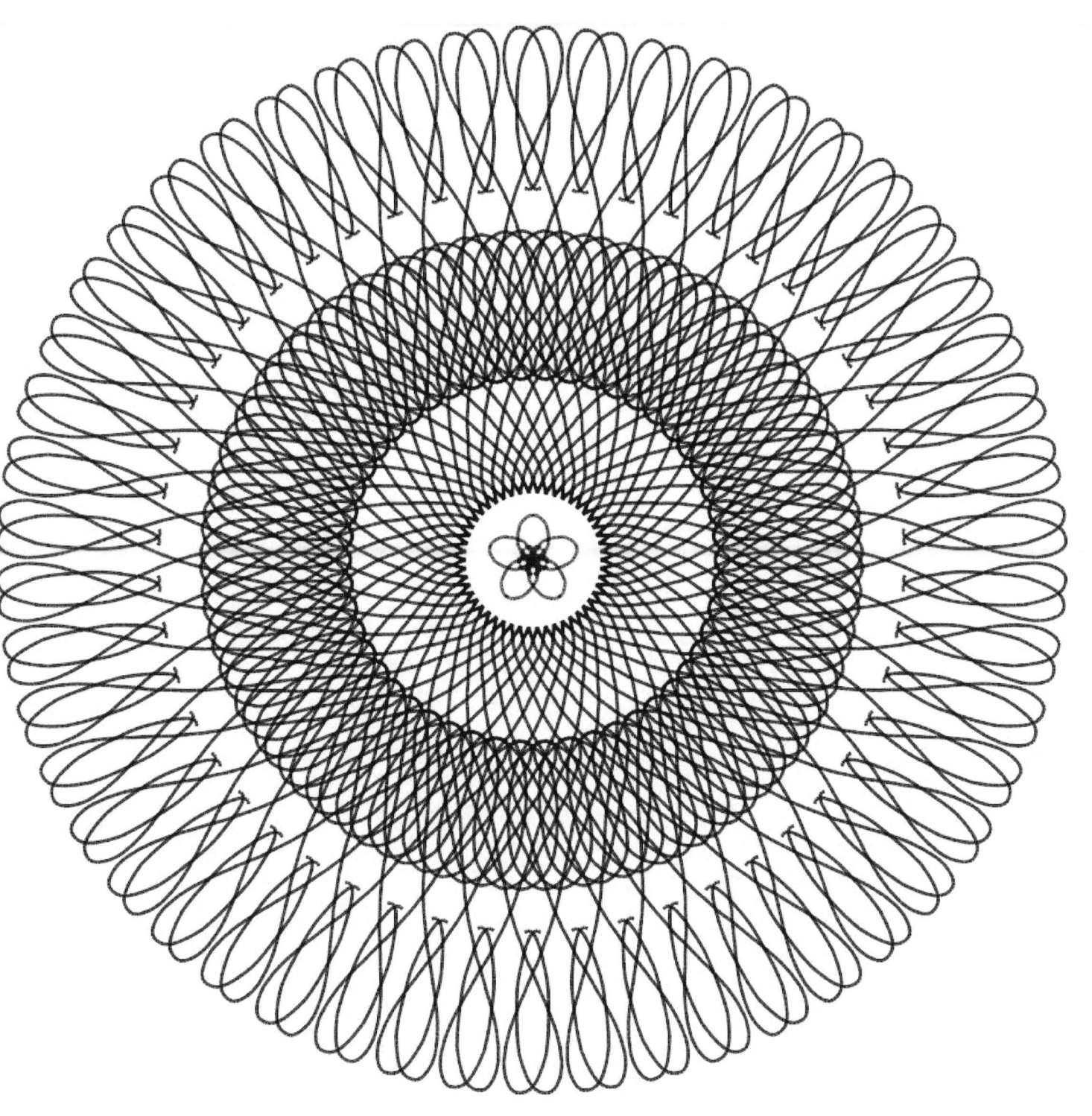

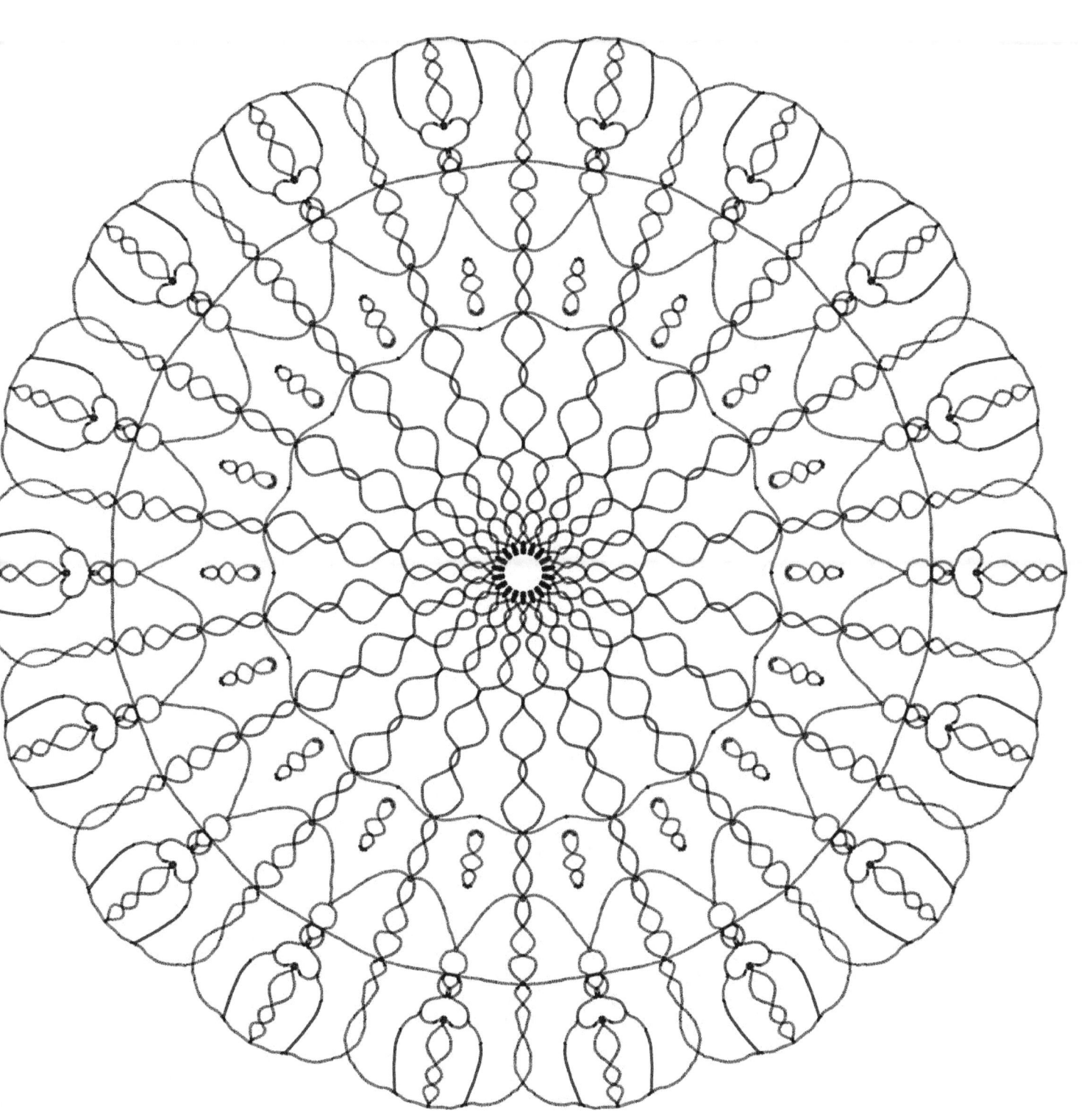

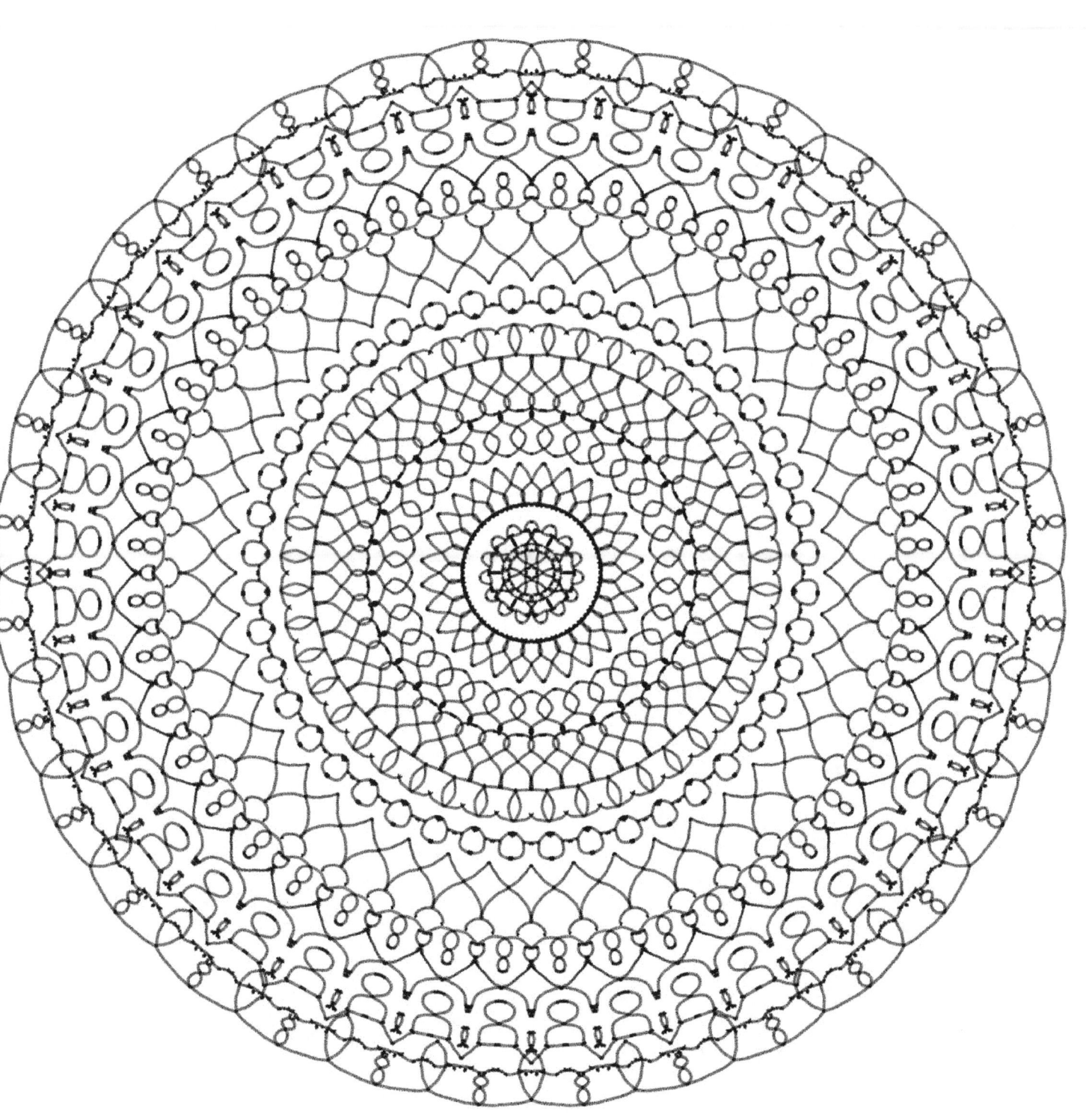

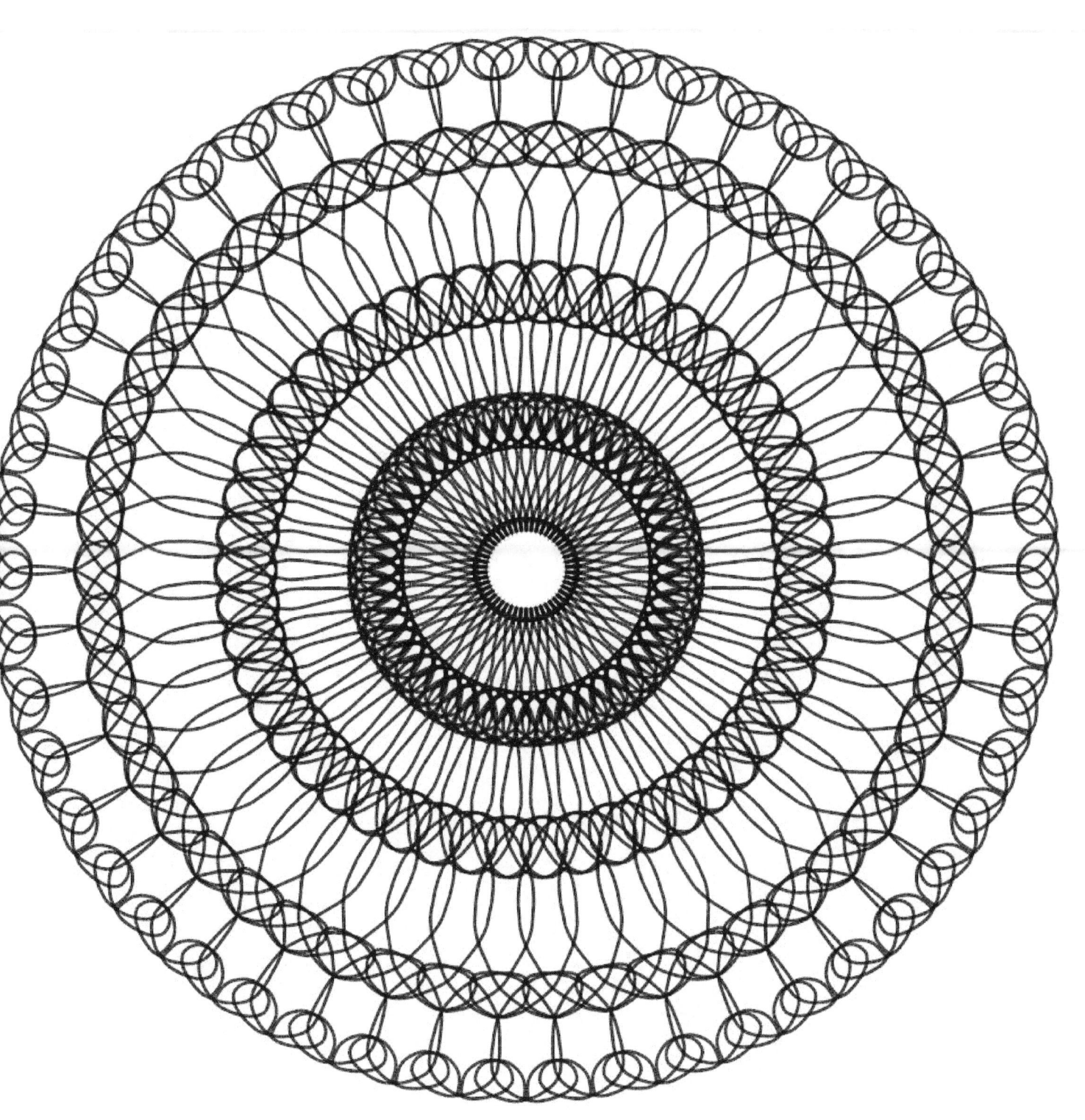

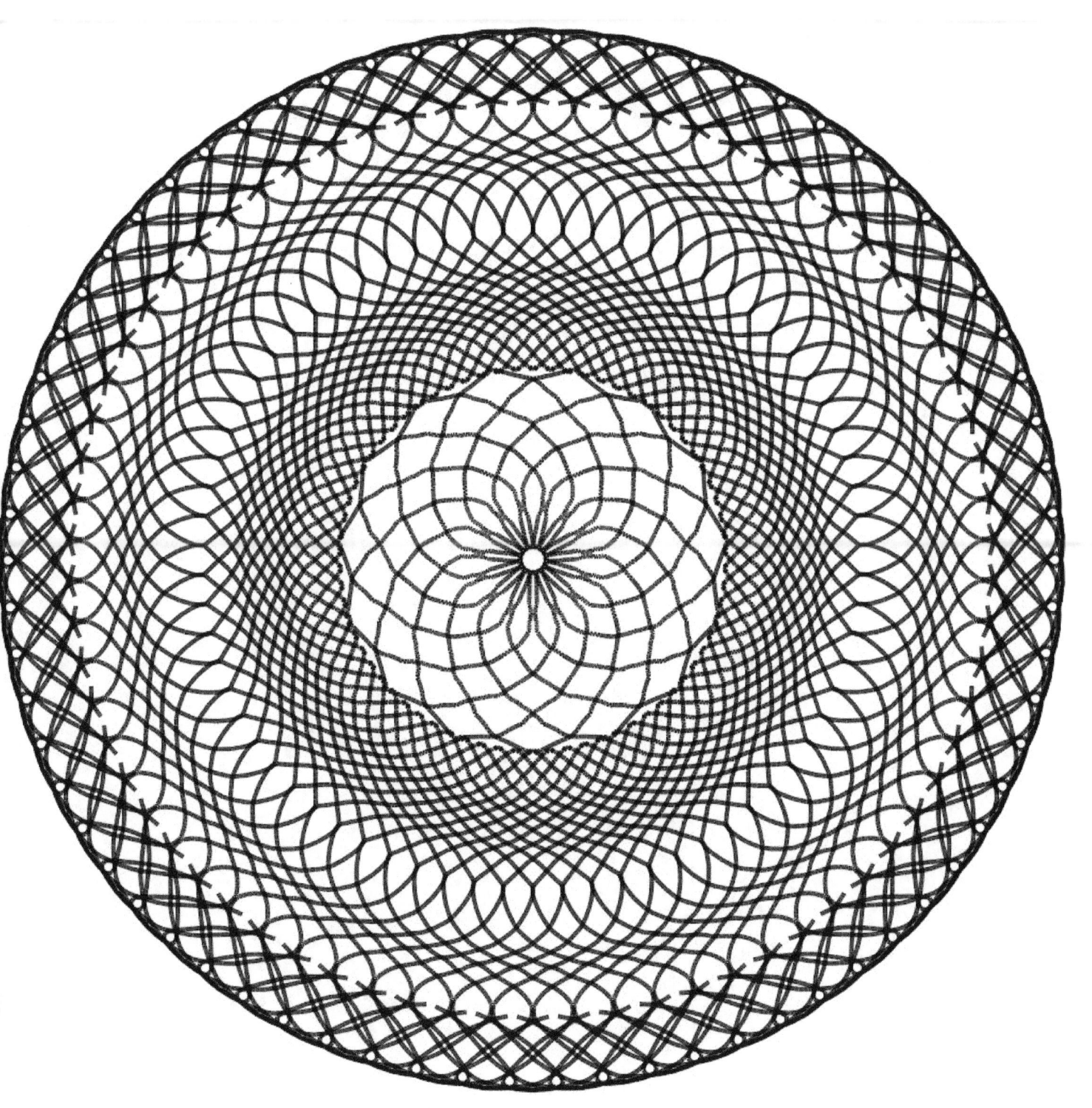

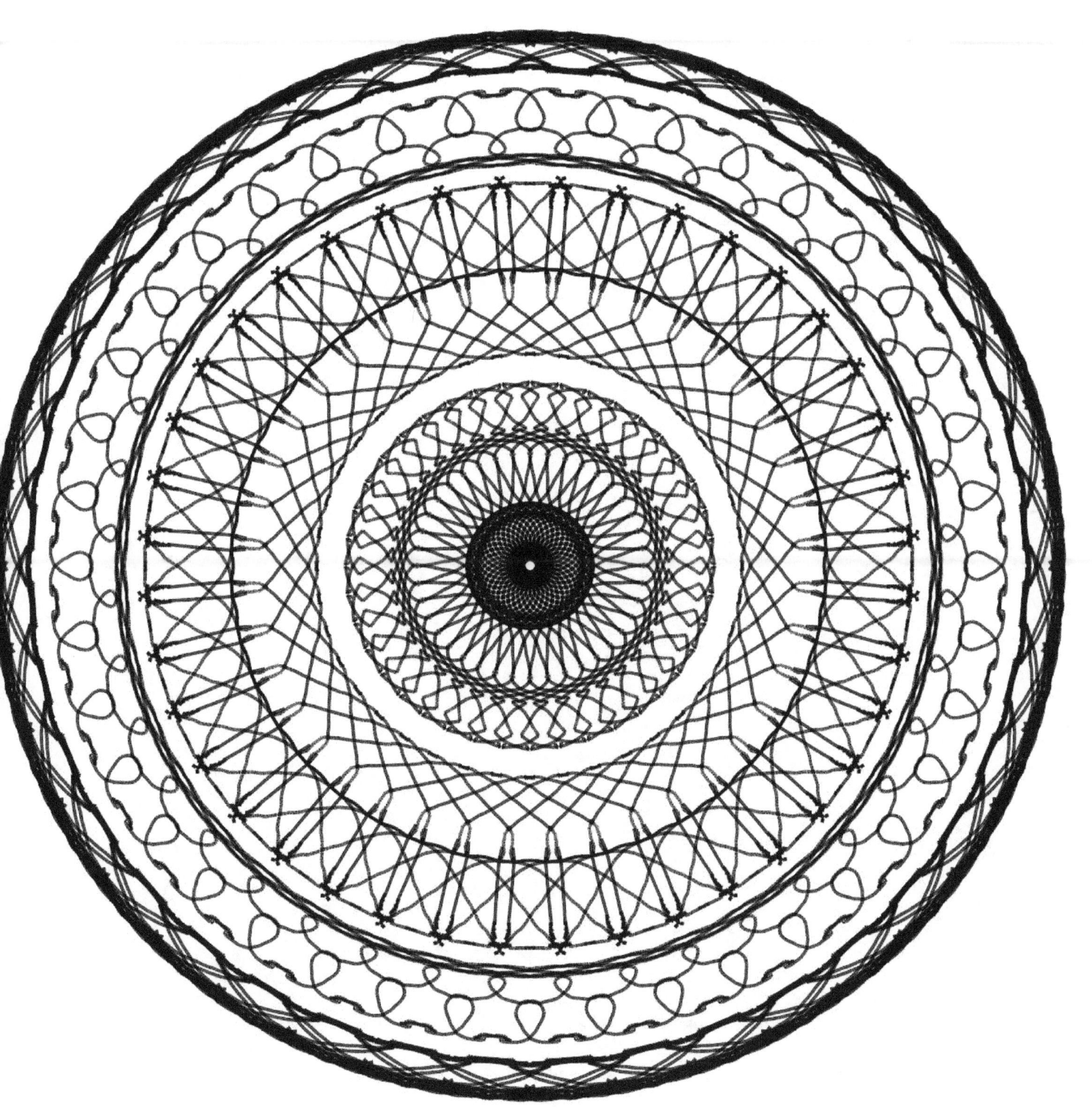

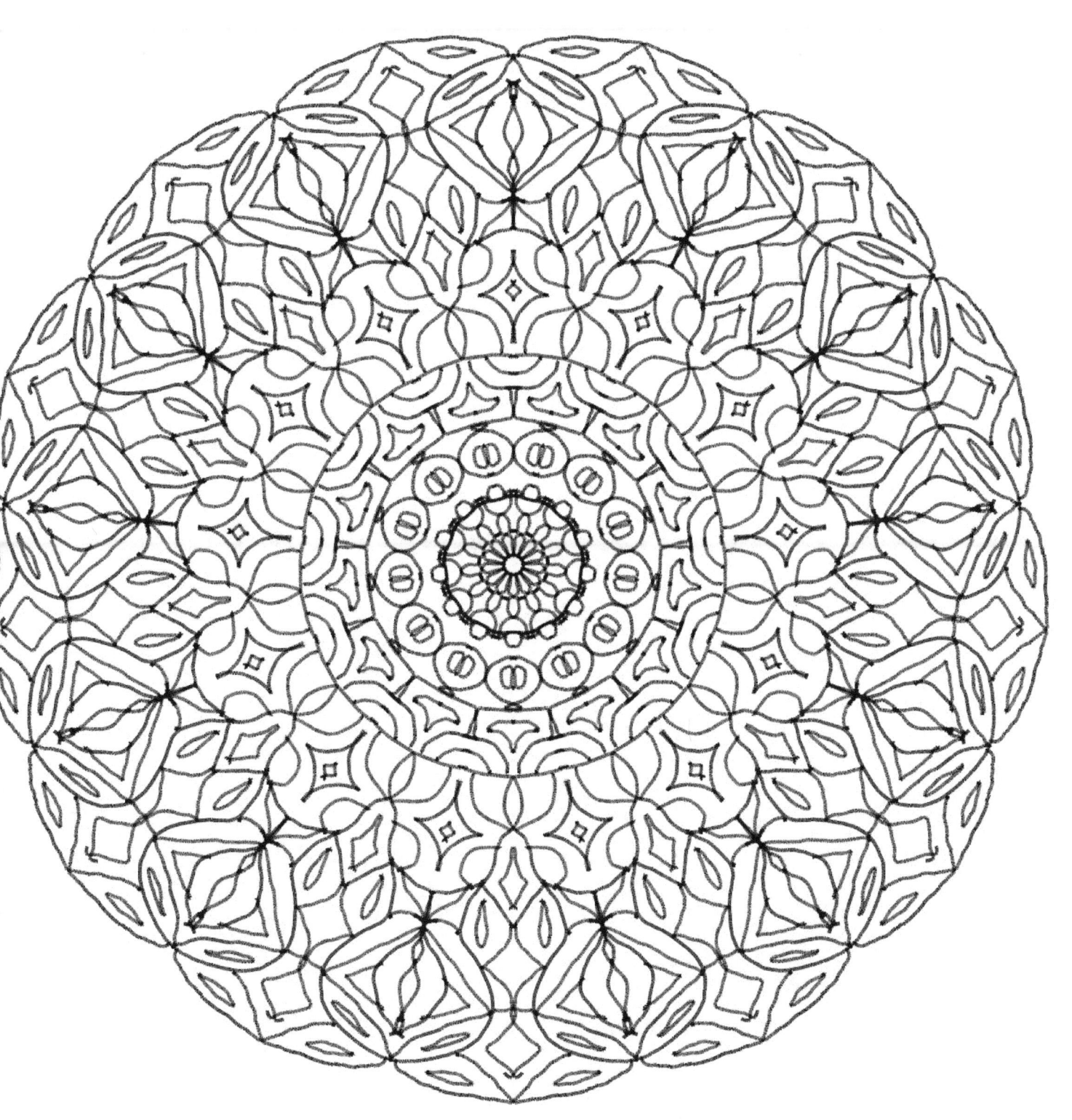

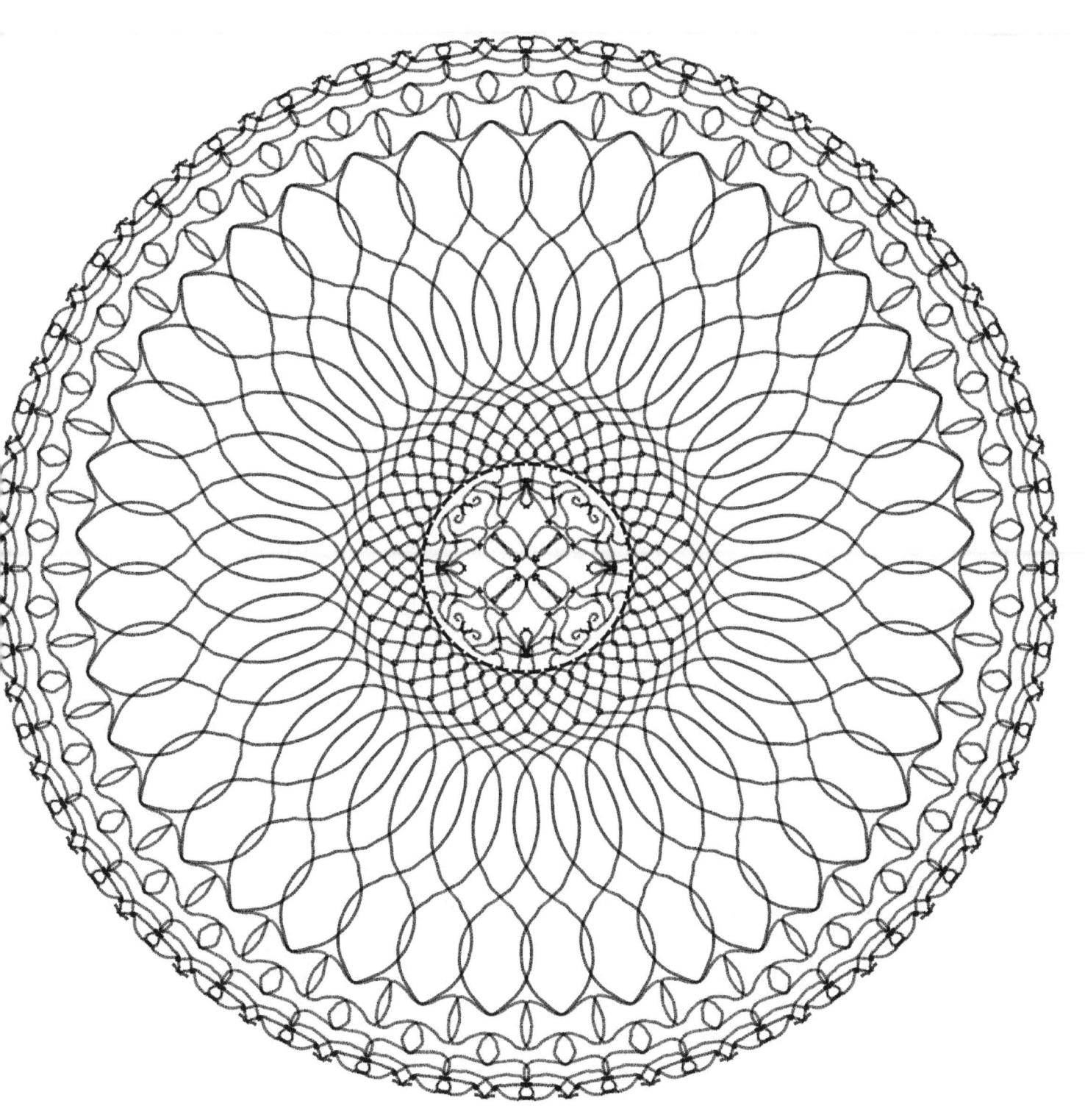

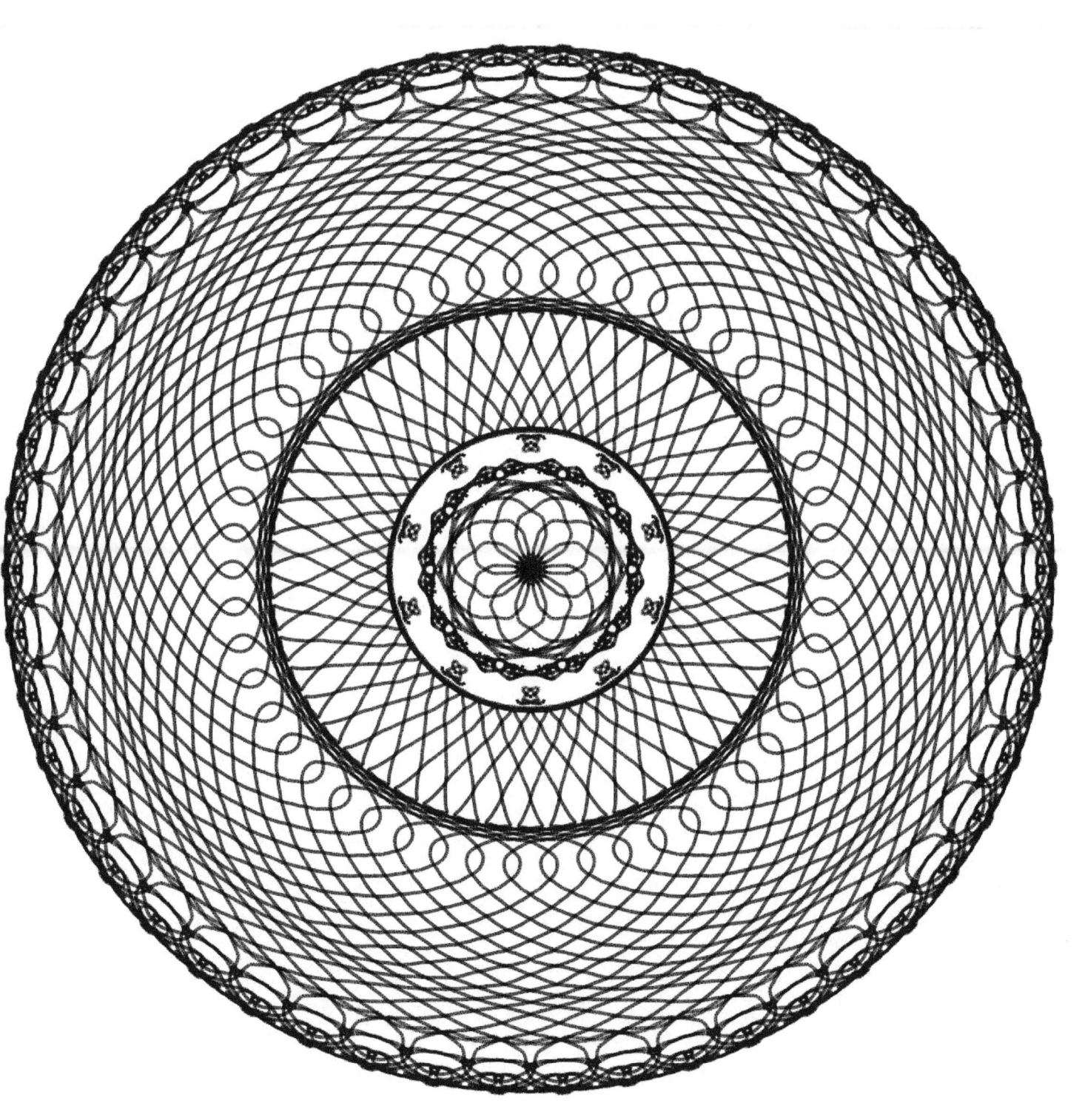

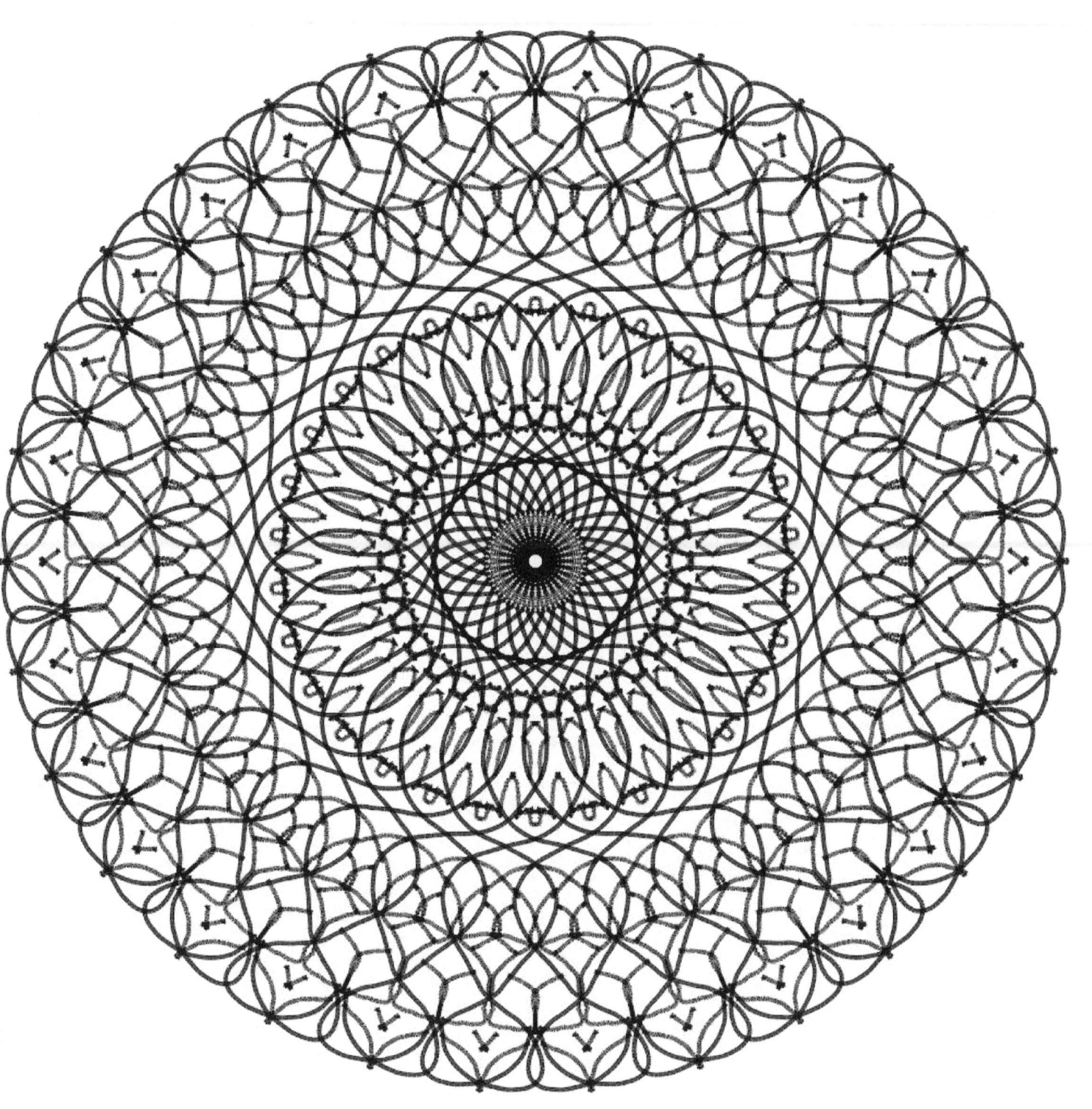

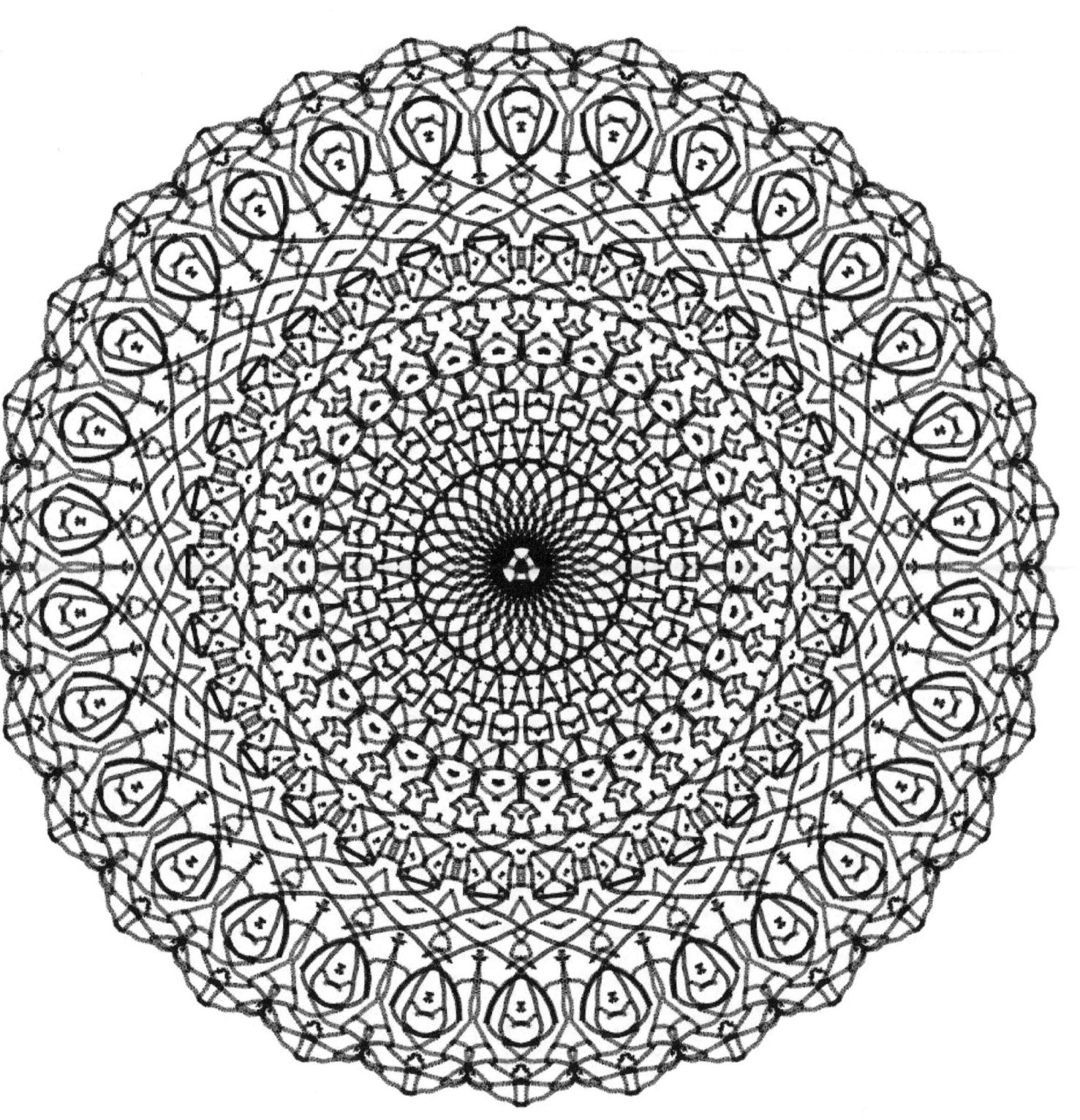

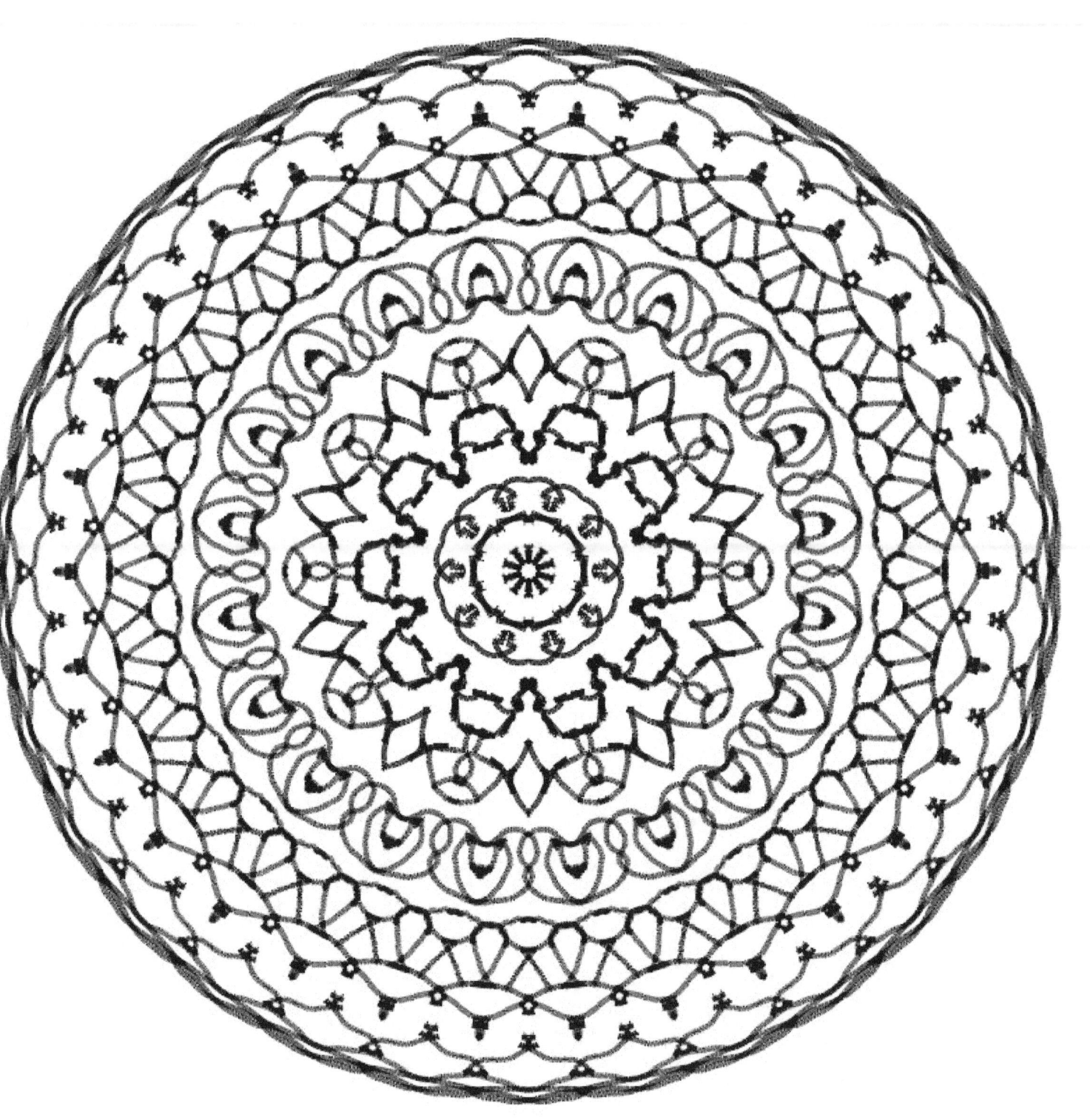

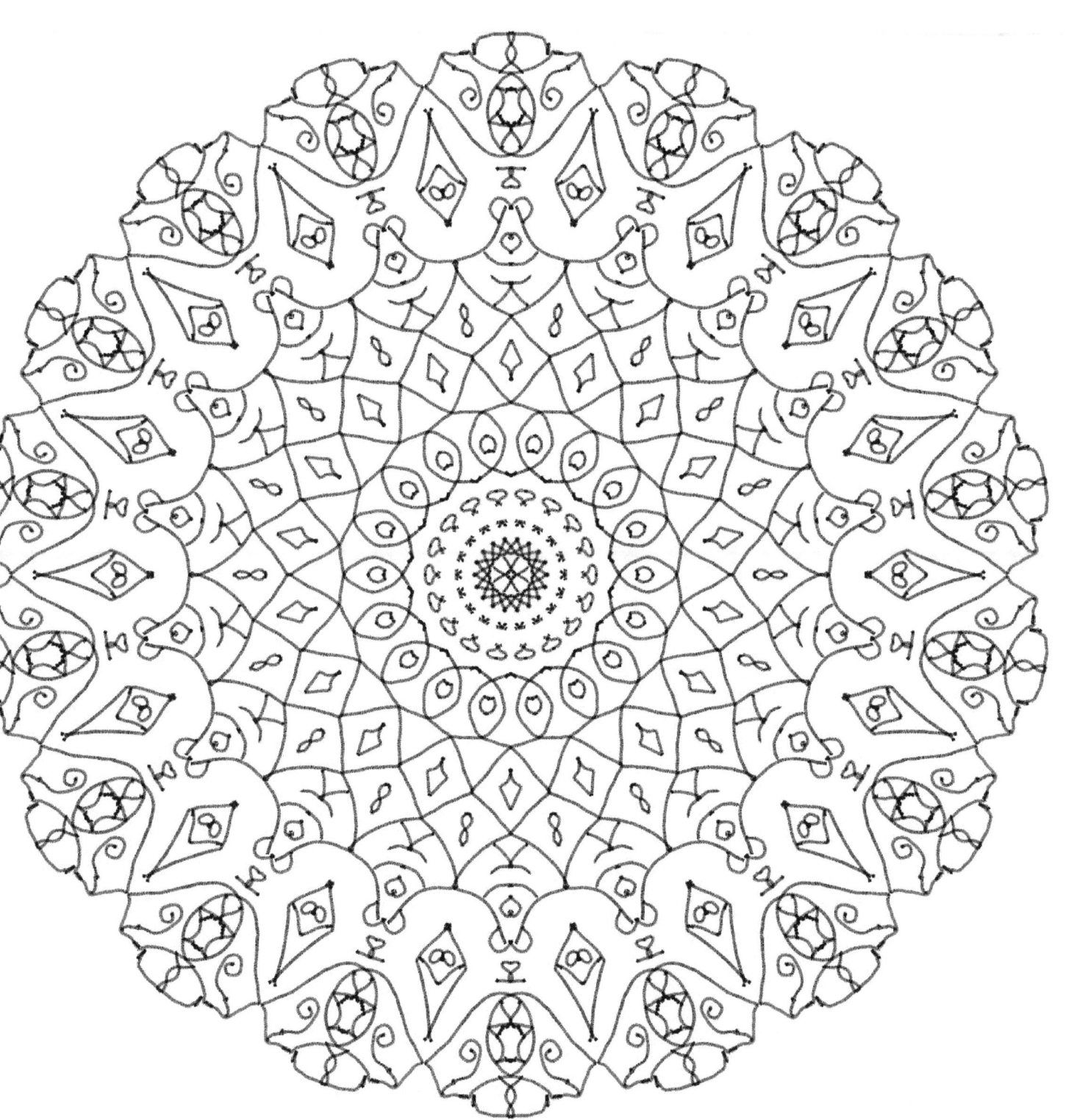

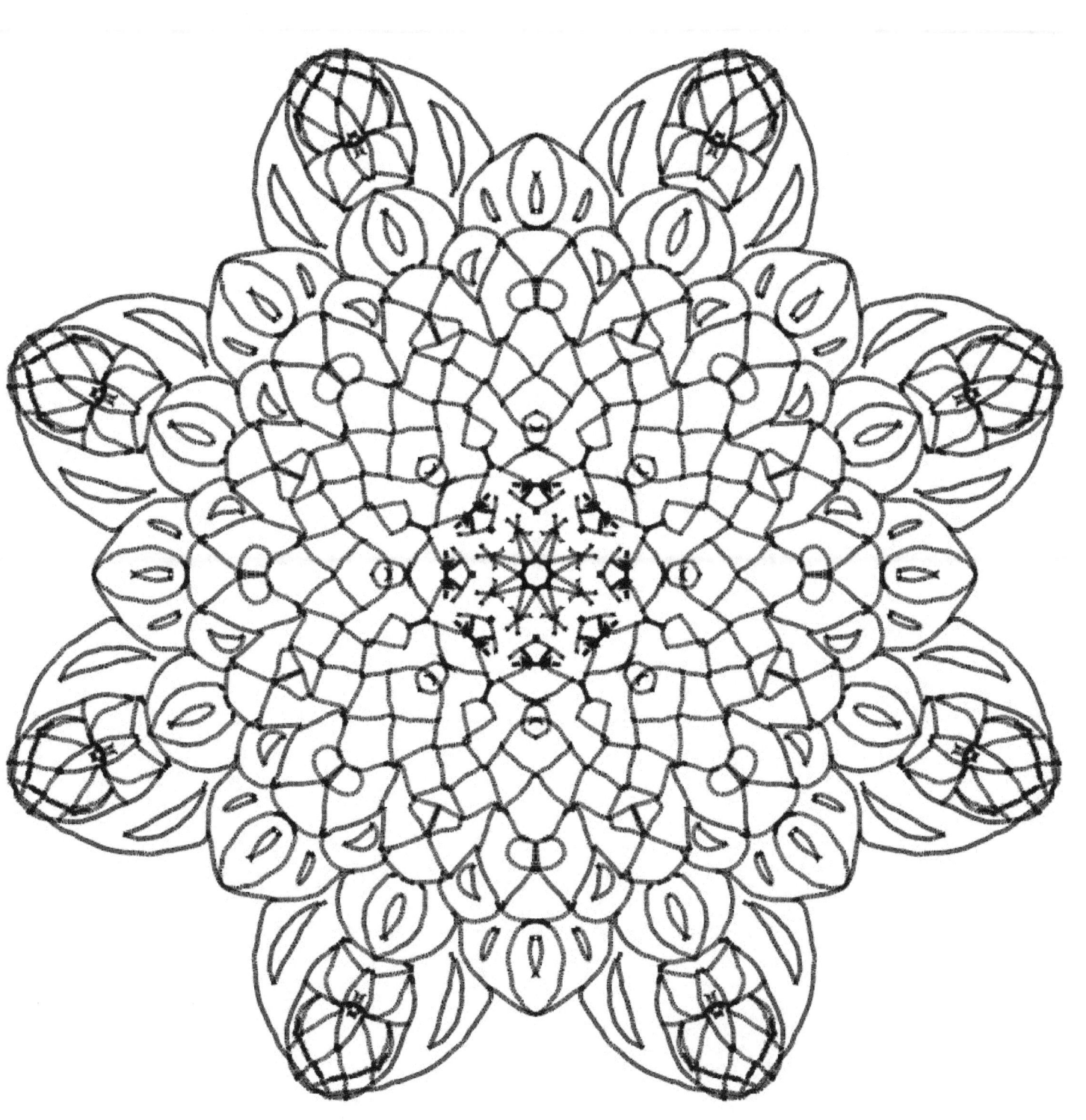

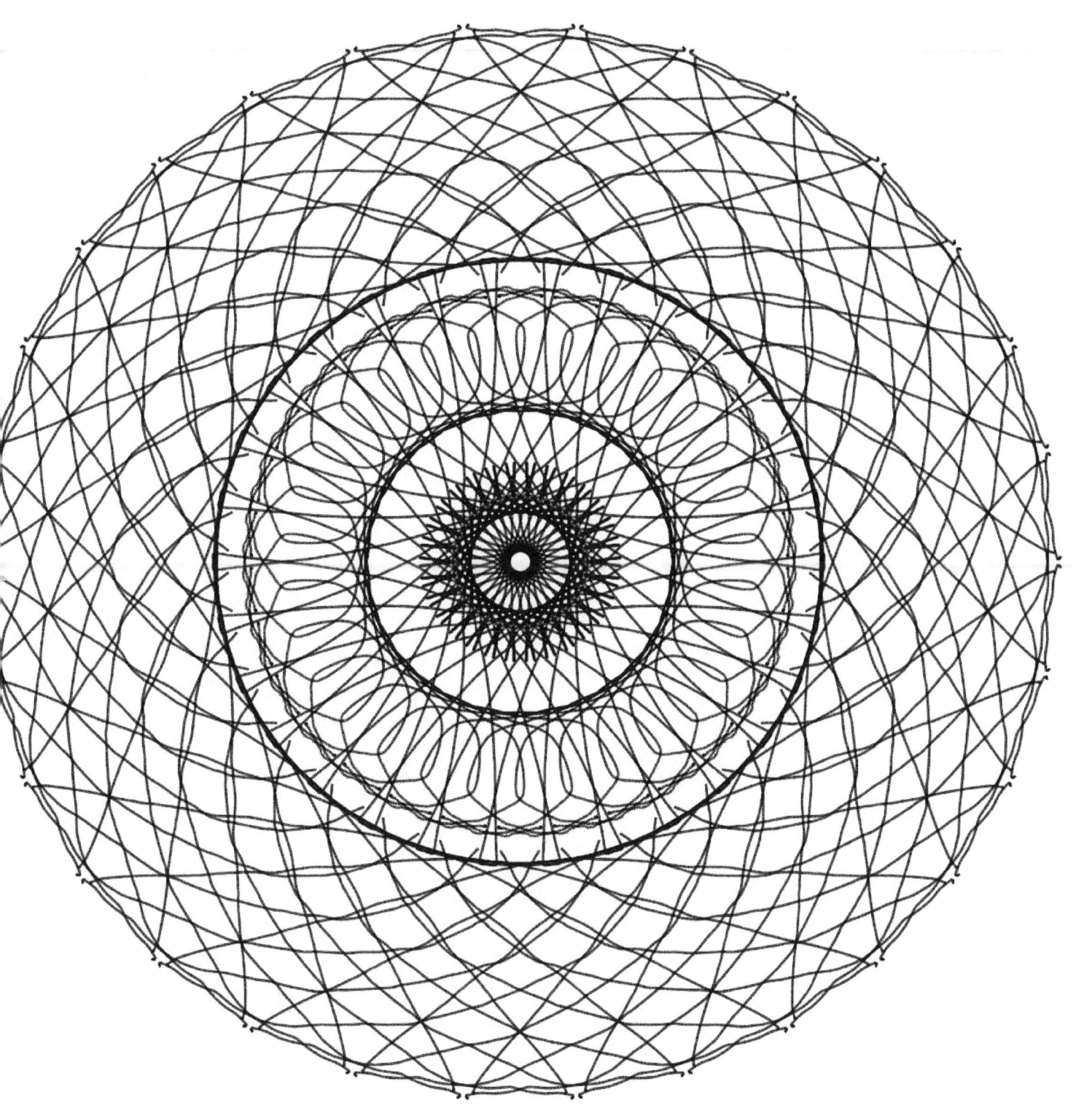

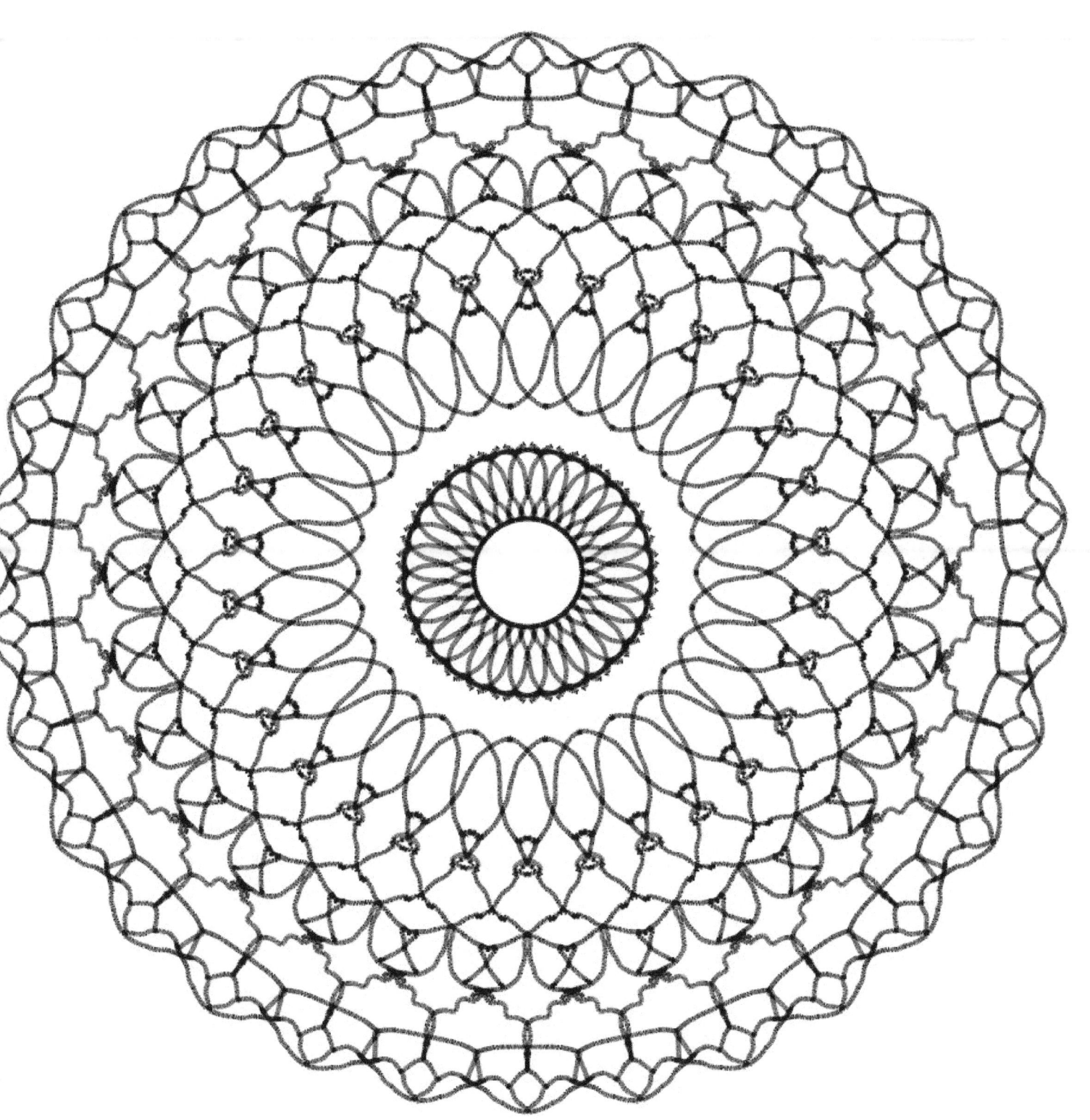

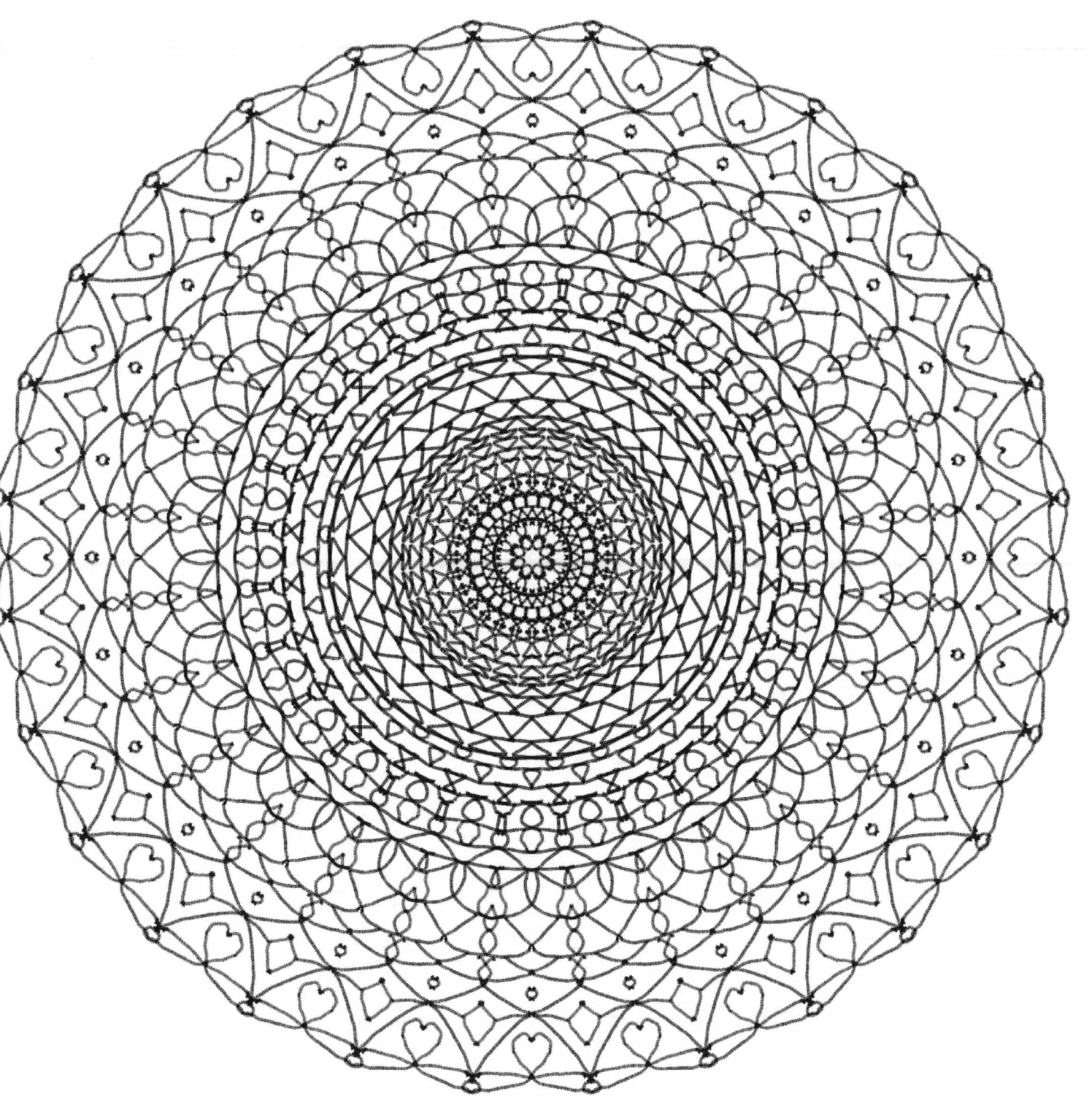

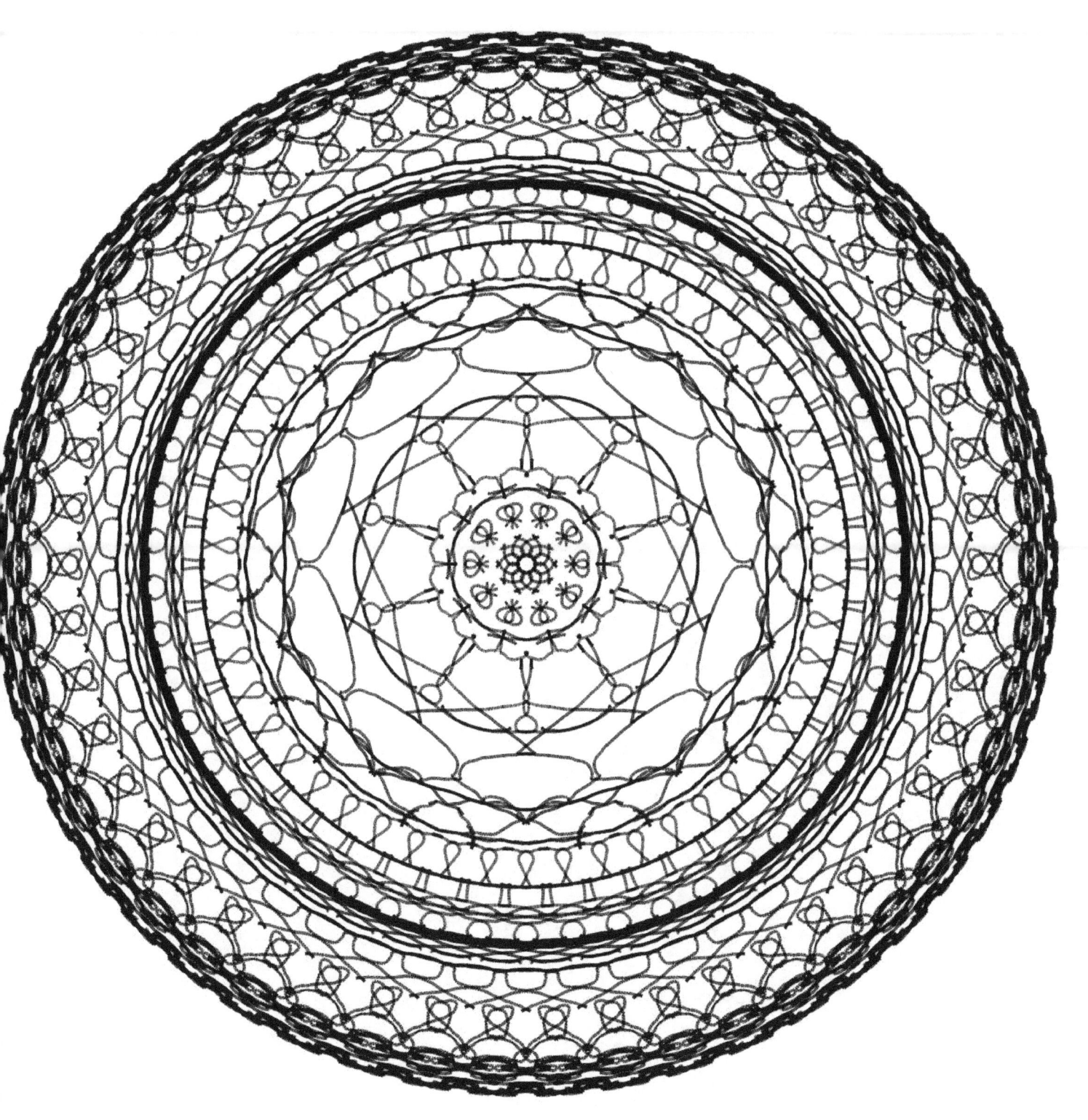

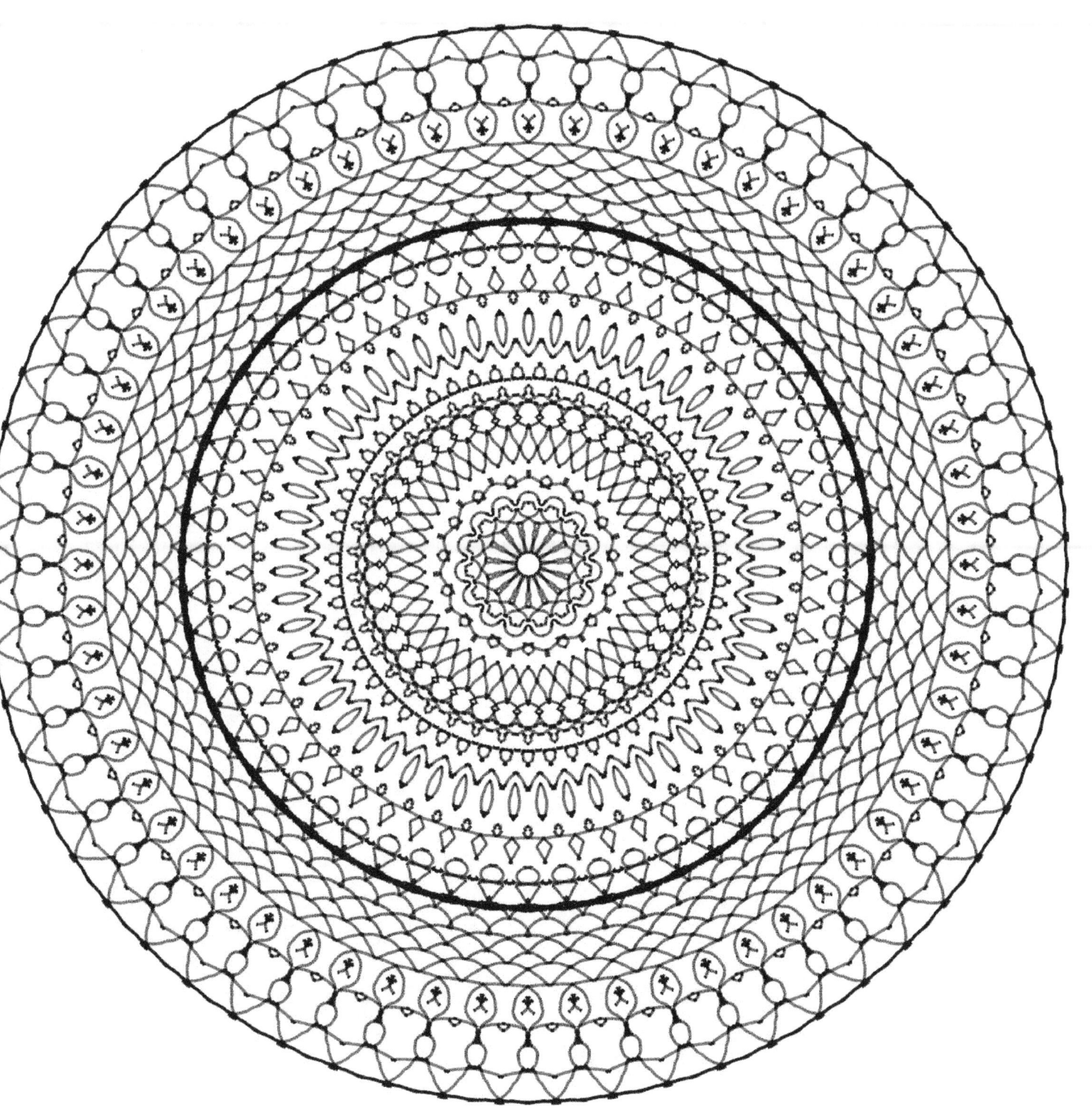

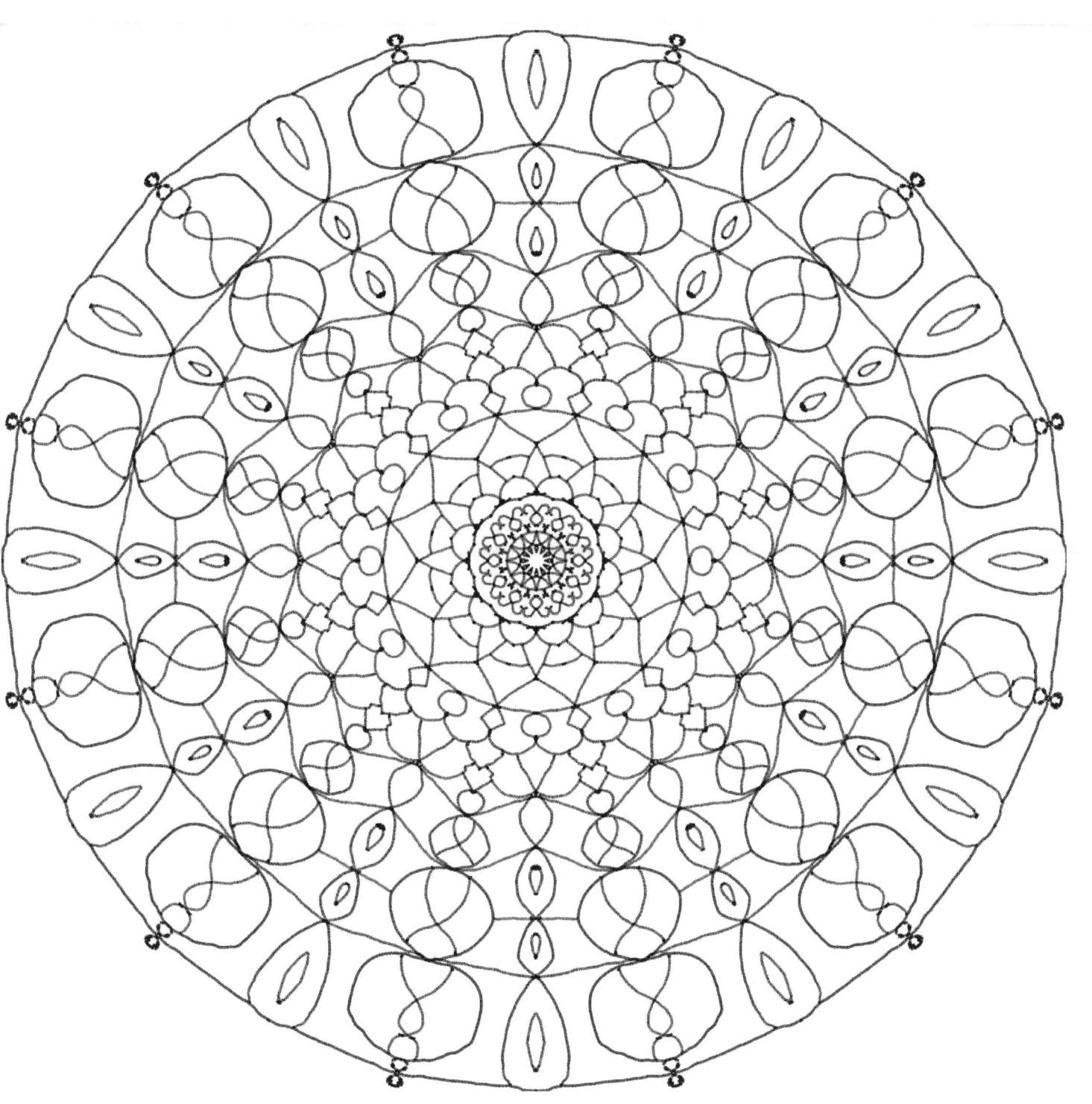

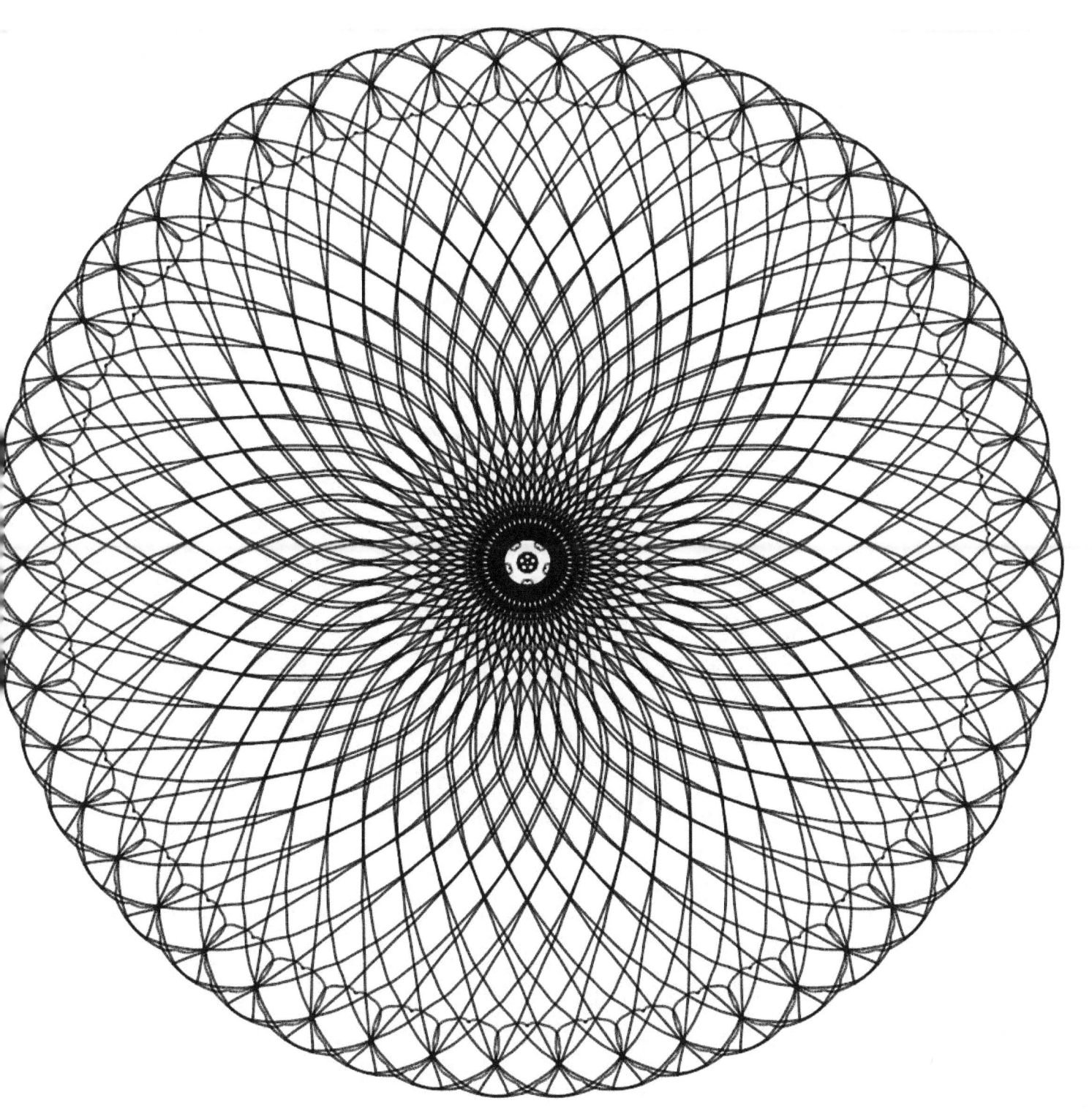

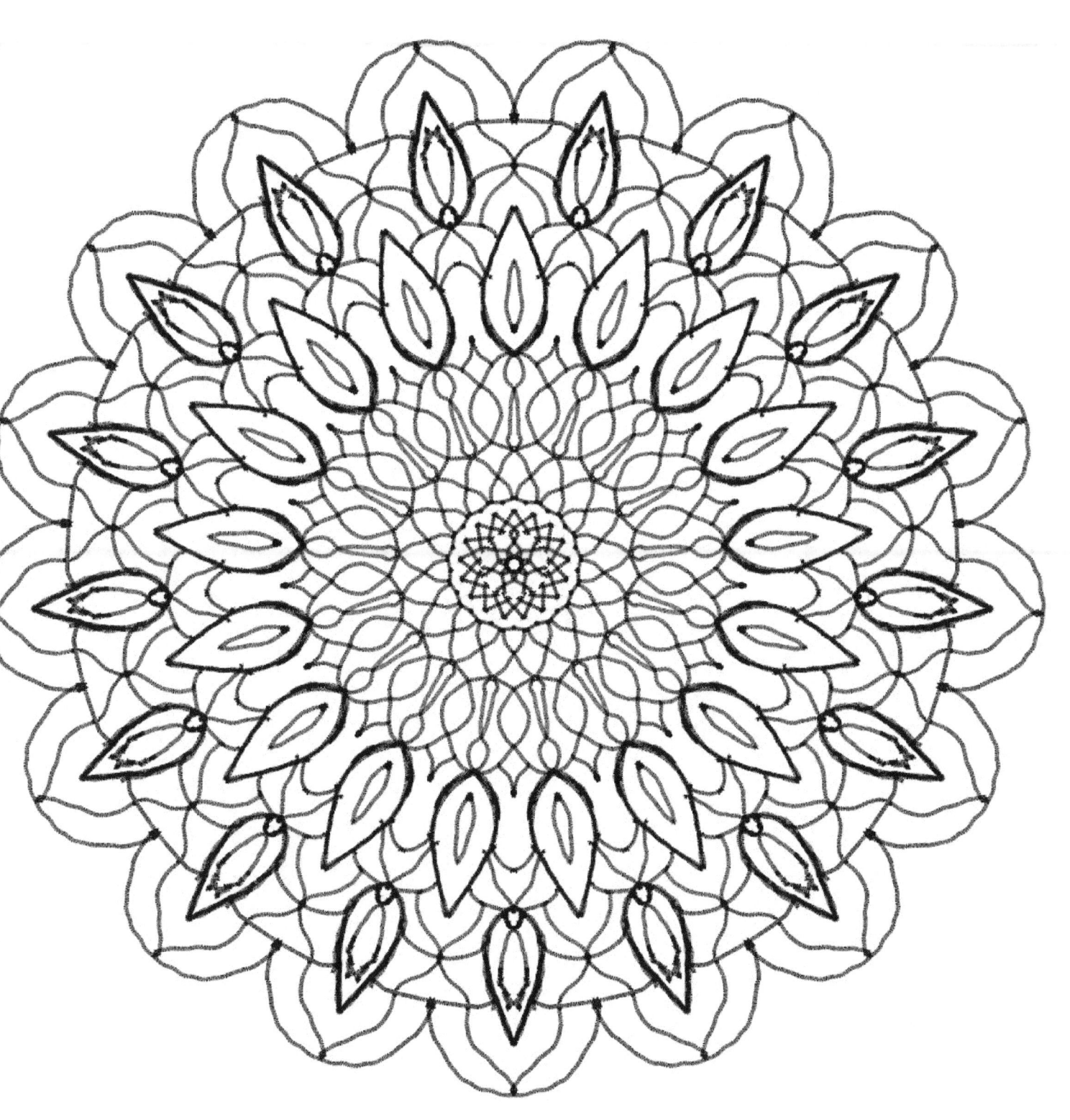

Namaste